People are talking about Tom Sirotnak and
Ultimate Warriors!

With this book, Tom Sirotnak doesn't become a role model for us men, but a hero. This is a book for men who aspire to be heroic.

Dr. Edwin Louis Cole, Founder, Christian Men's Network, Dallas, Texas

I'm tired of the devil kicking our behinds in this culture because God's team is still in the locker room. *Ultimate Warriors* challenges men of every age to assume Christian-based leadership. Tom Sirotnak gives men a creed to live by, a destiny to shoot for, and a mission to accomplish. Reading this book is dangerous to the devil's schemes, for it will raise up men who will do great exploits in furthering the Great Commission.

Darrell Green, All-Pro Defensive Back, Washington Redskins

It is unfortunate that some Christians are content with just making the team. *Ultimate Warriors* shows us that there is much more to it than that. Tom Sirotnak charges men to not only get in the game, but to play at a championship level. God is calling the men of this generation to get off the bench and make a difference for His kingdom. I encourage you to read this book.

Mark Brunnell, Quarterback, Jacksonville Jaguars

Jesus said, "Unless a man is born again, he cannot see the kingdom of God"; unfortunately, in the twentieth century we have made the object of the sentence "being born again." In *Ultimate Warriors,* Tom takes you into the real object of what Christ was talking about—the kingdom of God. This is must reading for those who want to get off the sideline and into the game.

Greg Ball, President, Champions for Christ, Austin, Texas

Ultimate Warriors is a hard-hitting, in-your-face challenge for Christian men to *really* make Jesus "Lord" of their lives. Tom fires on men who have become undisciplined, self-serving "couch potatoes" and issues a no-holds-barred mandate to become world changers, committed to carrying out the Great Commission with integrity and anointing.

Dr. Gary Greenwald, Pastor, Eagles Nest Ministries, Irvine, California

This book really got at my comfort zone. It challenged my total being to understand there is only one way, the cross. God knows our hearts and the time for playing games is over. There are so many lives at stake. We need to know we are called to fulfill our destiny. This book will hit you where you live. Get it, read it, and help shake the world.

Rosey Grier, Speaker, Author, & Former NFL All-Pro Lineman

Tom Sirotnak is one of a new breed of American champions who God is raising up for the twenty-first century. His no-nonsense call to excellence is reminiscent of the highly charged, pre-Super Bowl locker room challenges of the late, great Vince Lombardi. Tom's experiences . . . will deeply inspire you, lending a refreshing, new meaning to the term, "Christian."

Dr. Randall Parr, President, The Randall Parr Organization, Dallas, Texas

Ultimate Warriors delivers! It's a practical blueprint and training manual for those who want their manhood to count. If you're tired of surveying the neutered landscape of modern manhood and want to do something about it, get this book—and absorb it! Take the challenge of being one of God's "Ultimate Warriors!"

Al Manamtam, Senior Pastor, City Gate Christian Church, Honolulu, Hawaii

I have often said, "The most meaningless statistic in sports is the half-time score." So it is in our walk with God. It doesn't matter where you are in life now, but how you will finish. The theme of *Ultimate Warriors* is to birth champions for Christ who will fight long and finish strong! This is "must reading" for every man of God.

Meadowlark Lemon, The "Clown Prince" of Basketball's Harlem Globetrotters

Tom's life demonstrates what a warrior should be. *Ultimate Warriors* challenges all men to be men—men having true grit and conquering attitudes, hell-charging believers who know God's Word and are willing to say, "Yes, Lord, make me an ultimate warrior." This is what I want for myself and other men. What will it be for you?

Danny Jackson, Pastor, First Baptist Church, Morton, Texas

Fosdick said years ago that for too long we have sentimentalized Jesus in poetry, painting, and song. Jesus Christ was the ultimate warrior, a true champion and in a very real sense a never-say-die fighter for the souls of men. *Ultimate Warriors* tells us how we can be not only a warrior, but a champion.

Dave Diles, Pinehurst, North Carolina, Author & Former ABC Broadcaster

It is never enough to describe things from afar off. Tom Sirotnak's book, *Ultimate Warriors,* is cuttingly honest and spiritually instructional because it is written from pure experience. It is my desire that those who read this book would be inspired and challenged to engage the enemy and, in doing so, would develop their own experiences through participation in God's kingdom.

John Anderson, Pastor, First Baptist Church, Peaster, Texas

Men need to read *Ultimate Warriors.* This book will challenge and change a man so that he can become all God wants him to be. We need men to become "Ultimate Warriors" in today's world. I need to become an "Ultimate Warrior!"

Brian Harper, Coach, Scottsdale Christian Academy, Scottsdale, Arizona,
Former Major League Catcher

Tom's first book, *Warriors,* was a desperate call for men to get serious about Christ. *Ultimate Warriors* issues that same call along with sound biblical principles to assist the warrior along the path of true discipleship. You can feel Tom's passion for godly men with every story and application. I hope and pray that many Christians will read this book. The church today needs pews filled with ultimate warriors!

Gene Jennings, Pastor, First Baptist Church, Bath, South Carolina

Tom Sirotnak is a man on a mission. He brings to the playing field major league motivation. His methods are founded on godly character and integrity. *Ultimate Warriors* has to be on the "must read" list for anyone interested in going to the next level. You will be challenged, encouraged, and inspired as you read and adapt his life-changing principles.

Van Crouch, Author and President, Van Crouch Communications

Tom Sirotnak has been on the cutting edge of ministering into the lives of athletes and members of the body of Christ. As he hears the voice of God to bring a word in season, you can be reassured it's fresh manna from heaven that's life changing. I consider Tom a friend and an uncompromising man of God who can truly bring you up higher.

Reverend Dennis Tinerino, Four-time Mr. America-Mr. Universe

ULTIMATE WARRIORS

ULTIMATE WARRIORS

DARE TO SHAKE

YOUR WORLD

FOR CHRIST

TOM SIROTNAK
WITH KEN WALKER

BROADMAN
& HOLMAN
PUBLISHERS

Nashville, Tennessee

Published by Broadman & Holman Publishers, Nashville, Tennessee
Acquisitions & Development Editor: Vicki Crumpton
Printed in the United States of America

4260-81
0-8054-6081-0

Dewey Decimal Classification: 248.842
Subject Heading: MEN—RELIGIOUS LIFE
Library of Congress Card Catalog Number: 96-19244

Library of Congress Cataloging-in-Publication Data

Sirotnak, Tom, 1958–
    Ultimate warriors : dare to shake your world for Christ / Tom Sirotnak with Ken Walker.
        p.   cm.
    ISBN 0-8054-6081-0 (pb)
    1. Spiritual warfare. 2. Men—Religious life. 3. Men—Conduct of life.   I.
Walker, Ken, 1951–.
    BV4509.5S56   1996
    248.8'42—dc20

    96-19244
    CIP

96 97 98 99 00 5 4 3 2 1

John 15:13 says, "Greater love has no one than this, that one lay down his life for his friends." In a world of disposable relationships, half-hearted convictions, and broken promises, it is rare to find a loyal friend who will stick closer than a brother. I have been extremely fortunate to find a family of such friends. We are locked arm in arm as colaborers and soldiers in God's army. This book is dedicated to those who pursue with me God's command to occupy until Jesus returns:

- To my wife, Dana, the sweetest woman in the world. Your undying love and commitment is the strength behind all I will ever do. I love you!

- To our children—Stephen Rice, Tommy Jr., and Sharon Rose, and (God willing) Cody Edward—the future warriors and champions for Christ. Never forget God has a destiny for you. May God's wisdom, power, and grace be with you. You will always be my greatest treasure.

- To pastor Phil Bonasso, Rice Broocks, Greg Ball, and all my brethren at MorningStar Ministries International, and my fellow warriors in Champions for Christ. Keep training Christian leaders. Never give up the good fight of faith.

- To my brothers and staff on the Power Team: leader and founder, John Jacobs, and his wife, Ruthanne; Mike Hagen (whose son, Mike Jr., inspired this book's title); Berry Handley; Eddie "The Gripper" Dalcour; Siolo Tauaefa; the Keenan Smith family; Clarence "Mookie" Lee; Smiley Elmore; Jeff Neal; Todd Keene; Jaime Coronado; Mickey Hensley; and special recognition to Brandon Hensley. Our fellowship has been sweet. You have been tremendous examples of courage, faith, and personal sacrifice. I am honored to have been part of such a fine team.

- To my mom and dad, Gloria and Ed Sirotnak; my brother, Eddie Jr.; and my mother- and father-in-law, Joan and Robert Cody. You have been there for me and my family every step of the way. For this, I thank you. I am blessed to have such a wonderful family. I love you all.

- To my "extended" family: Al and Para Manamtam and their sweet daughter, Shannon; Jack and Diana Mondonedo and their future world changer, Jarred; Mario and Gina Gonzales and their two sons of thunder, Alex and Aaron; the Glen Hamilton family; the White house—Eric, Kim, and Madison; Jim and Shellie Burton; Danny and Lisa Strand; Lakita Garth; Brenda Petesch; Gabriela and Margie Licon; Kristen Blalock; Steve Hauser; Crestine Villanueva; the Bonasso clan—Phil, Karen, Amber, Kimberly, Pamela, Rebecca, and Candice; my "boys" Tony Fetchel, Franc Garcia, Charlie Coons, and Reggie Pendleton; and my all-time champ, A. C. Green. (Please forgive me if I left anyone out.) You have laid down your lives in service to our family and ministry. I anxiously await the testimonies the Lord will work through each of you. May you see your ten thousand where I have seen my one thousand!

- To Edwin Louis Cole and his Christian Men's Network. I respect you as an international pioneer for the men's movement. More important personally, you have mentored me in masculinity. The patterns, principles, and promises from God's Word that you imparted to me flow throughout the pages. May you be rightfully credited as an active participant with all those who would be touched and changed through the teachings of this book. You will always be a hero to me and my family. We love you.

- To Ken Walker, my coauthor and trusted friend. May God bless you and launch you into a new sphere of influence through your writings. The best is yet to come (see Zech. 4:6–7).

Coauthor's Dedication

To my father, David, whose living example showed me what it means to be a man; to my brother, Dennis, who kept his faith when I walked away from mine; and to my wife, Janet, whose strong faith and earnest seeking of God inspire me each day.

Contents

Foreword

With the increased feminization of the Western male in general, and the Western church in particular, the Holy Spirit has been moving powerfully to help Christian men discover biblical manhood. This has not been easy. The church is surrounded by a culture that promotes the extremes of the "macho" man or the effeminate, "sensitive" male. *Ultimate Warriors* will help readers rediscover the model of manhood that Jesus clearly established.

Like countless thousands of other Christian men, Tom Sirotnak senses a stirring to accept the challenge and make the journey toward our heavenly Father's portrait of real manhood. With crystal-clear vision, he points us to the only picture that has ever been free of sin's distortion: Jesus Christ. The Ultimate Warrior, the Lion of Judah and the Lamb of Heaven, emerges in this book as the only true hero for both men and women. He made them, and He alone knows how they were created to be fulfilled and righteous in every situation.

In a world weary of meaningless words, bankrupt theories, shallow sound bites, and empty slogans, those searching for the real thing demand living examples. Hearts cry out, "Show me, don't tell me." Tom's awareness that reality is in seeing shines through this book. Filled with numerous personal illustrations and real people who have experienced struggles and victories, *Ultimate Warriors* is a breath of fresh air.

Knowing Tom personally, I can vouch for the intensity of his struggle for biblical manhood and the courageous example of his evangelistic zeal. As I read the chapters of this book, I was repeatedly inspired by Tom's examples of courageous men. I know many of them personally too. I can vouch for their integrity and assure you that Tom is not taking "evangelistic" liberties in describing their successes and failures.

I enjoyed many of his insights into Scripture and appreciate the necessity for this book and others that I am sure will follow. However, what I appreciate most is Tom himself. A watershed incident that speaks loudly about his character occurred several years ago. Tom picked me up from the airport in Los Angeles, where I was to speak at a conference. The rainy fall weather had made the freeways into a slicky-slide nightmare. Suddenly in the rear view mirror Tom saw a car careening madly toward us. Smashing the accelerator, he tried desperately to avoid the crash but to no avail. After making sure I was all right, he jumped out to check on the other motorist.

Although the large man looked frightened, he was OK. But he had a squirrelly look in his eye. It seemed apparent he had no insurance or some other reason to flee the scene at the first opportunity. I wondered how "Big Tommy" would handle it—with threats, intimidation, or maybe by laying a few heavy Scriptures on him. Instead, Tom simply commanded, "Don't leave." The driver obeyed. Tom's firmness, mixed with respect and humanity, deeply impressed me. It wasn't just his size that carried the day. It was the genuineness of his authority.

As men like Ed Cole and groups like Promise Keepers step in to meet the current manhood crisis, I am sure that Christ will help us all to grasp His humanity and maleness in a way that will set us free. I'm equally certain that Tom Sirotnak will be making his own significant contribution. May you enjoy this book to the point of inspiration. Others across the centuries already have feasted on the heart of its message: "Those who do wickedly against the covenant he shall corrupt with flattery; . . . the people who know their God shall be strong, and carry out great exploits" (Dan. 11:32, NKJV).

—Dennis Peacocke, Founder
Strategic Christian Services
Santa Rosa, California

Introduction

HOW DID HE
DO THAT?

I am a little embarrassed to admit how many times I saw *Forrest Gump*. Let's just say it was more than twice. Analyzing its broad appeal, social commentators attributed its popularity to droves of baby boomers revisiting the turbulent 1960s and '70s. For me, the attraction was the special effects. As the movie showed scene after scene of Forrest with presidents and famous personalities, I asked my friends, "How did they do that? How did they make it look like he was actually meeting those people?"

I consulted all the "techies" I knew, but each one put a little different spin on the explanation. Then I saw an advertisement for the video, *The Making of "Forrest Gump."* Seizing the opportunity, I watched the video and took a tour through the amazing world of special effects and trick photography. Needless to say, all my questions were answered.

Obviously, this book isn't about making movies, but the making of spiritual warriors for Christ. When I observe the lives of *real* heroes, the same question burns in my mind—*How did they do that?* As much as I enjoy hearing the inspiring stories of *what* someone has done for God, I want to learn *how* they did it. *Ultimate Warriors* fits that description. Far from being a highlight film of some spiritual superstar (or a book about a professional wrestler), it contains the blueprint for making a champion.

Having known Tom Sirotnak (or as his friends call him, "Big Tommy") since the beginning of his Christian life,* I can tell you the things you are about to read are true. I remember a student who read the New Testament and quipped, "Nobody lives this way anymore." Big Tommy does. He has refused to be kept off the playing field of God's purposes. His life is his message, because he is an *Ultimate Warrior.*

Cut to the Chase

In reading a book like this, many seek the quickest, easiest path to the promised land. I found myself looking for "three easy steps to becoming incredible for Christ." But when it comes to spiritual greatness, someone once said, "If it was easy, then everyone would do it." While *Ultimate Warriors* offers no quick fixes, it presents proven principles. If followed faithfully, they will lead you into a lifestyle of victory.

The most important thing for a person who wants to become a champion for Christ is to build a strong foundation. This is especially critical in light of the ever-changing uncertainties of modern life. It is an understatement to say that the culture around us has become openly hostile to the Christian faith. Society says, "Sure, you can be a Christian, as long as you keep your beliefs to yourself. But if you start preaching in public, get ready for a fight."

Room 911

You must have the kind of foundation that can withstand a spiritual hurricane of opposition. Jesus said, "Everyone who comes to Me, and hears My words, and acts upon them . . . is like a man building a house,

*Rice Broocks led author Tom Sirotnak to Jesus on January 14, 1982, while Tom was attending USC.

who dug deep and laid a foundation upon the rock" (Luke 6:47–48). Christ pointed out that that house stands when the storms come. But, He added, the foolish man who hears His words and fails to act on them is like the man who builds his house without a foundation. The storm wipes him out. The large number of spiritual calamities for such a man reveals his inadequate foundation.

However, laying a foundation is not that exciting. Who wants to work so hard on something that will never be seen? Well, once your building is complete it will make a great difference. Bad foundations show up through cracks in the walls and ceilings. The cracks warn that something isn't right. Shortcuts at the bottom make for disasters on top.

I once took a team of students to the island of Guam for an evangelistic outreach. I should have known that something was amiss when they handed me my room key at the hotel: "Sir, your room number is 911." Everyone joked how we would be getting all the emergency calls. Little did we realize that we soon would be the ones in trouble.

Two days later, one of the century's worst earthquakes—8.2 on the Richter scale—hit the island. Even more incredible, it lasted for sixty quivering, gut-wrenching, fear-riveting seconds. As we sat in room 911, it seemed to explode. The television set hurtled to the floor. Slammed from its perch, the sliding glass door shattered into a million slivers. We ran for the fire escape, but that route was blocked.

Not knowing where else to go, we stood on the balcony to ride out the most terrifying minute of our lives. As each second ticked by, we felt certain that the building would collapse. Just as it felt like the hotel would rip in half, all motion ceased. We ran down the steps into the street and began singing praises to God. I never had an easier time telling strangers about the Lord!

The next day we toured the island to assess the damage. What stuck out was a new hotel on the verge of collapse. Two floors had disintegrated and the rest of the structure tilted like the Leaning Tower of Pisa. It looked solid before the quake, but the shaking revealed the faulty workmanship. The hotel had to be torn down. I couldn't help comparing that razed structure to our accommodations. As much as I give God the glory for saving our lives, I also thank the engineers who built the hotel, particularly the ones who laid the foundation. They appreciated the instability of an earthquake zone, so they built the foundation strong enough, yet with enough flexibility, to take the worst shaking. Apparently the builders of the other hotel took shortcuts.

How irresponsible it is not to take account of the "fault line" we are living on in this generation. Sin has warped the entire cosmos. Everywhere we see massive upheaval. We cannot simply lay any foundation: "For no man can lay a foundation other than the one which is laid, which is Jesus Christ" (1 Cor. 3:11). We must dig down deep and tear out everything that is hostile to Christ.

In the past decade we have seen many visible Christian pastors, leaders, and artists fall. We stand before the ruins, asking, "Why?" Later, after a spiritual autopsy, we discover there was never a solid foundation in the person's life. Sure, they *believed* in Jesus, but they had no real understanding of repentance or His lordship. Many of these casualties were never taught the need to open their lives to fellow believers who could challenge them and stand with them during times of temptation. Who knows what disasters could have been prevented if there had been "building inspectors" examining the foundations.

Ultimate Warriors will give you a look at the glorious difference a strong foundation makes. At the time of Tom's conversion to Christ, it was apparent he didn't intend to lead a double life. He was completely transparent. Most important, he was teachable. Second Timothy 3:16 says the Word of God is profitable "for teaching, for reproof, for correction, for training in righteousness." We all like the teaching part, but we're not too thrilled about the reproof and correction part.

But the latter is where the men are separated from the boys. Better yet, where the winners are separated from the losers. Who is willing to let the Lord reprove and correct him through other men? This shouldn't be so difficult. Individuals who want to be great athletes, pianists, gymnasts, scientists—you name it—learn from others teaching and correcting them. So it must be with the sons of Light.

Most would say we are living in the greatest time in human history. Technology has drawn the world so tightly together that we can realistically hope to preach to everyone who is open to the gospel. Yet, with all the opportunity that is before us, the challenge remains for us not to present a Christianity that is weak and anemic.

The early church turned their world upside down, with no TV, Internet, or supersonic jets—not even a sound system. What spoke to pagans was the reality that Christ had made new men and women out of those who truly followed Him. The disciples were able to withstand the pressure of the entire Roman Empire that came crashing down on them. They were "Ultimate Warriors," ready to lay down their lives for the cause of Jesus Christ. Let us pray that a new generation of such warriors rises up and pledges their all, so that our world will turn back to righteousness.

—Rice Broocks, International Director
MorningStar Ministries
Nashville, Tennessee

1

THE POWER
OF A GREAT CHALLENGE

*Don't let someone else create your own world for you, for when they do,
they will always make it too small.*

—Dr. Edwin Louis Cole

I sauntered into the gym with a broad smile, anticipating my daily
workout. Grunts sounded from a few hulks bench-pressing a hundred pounds more than their weight. The pungent odor of sour sweat
saturated the air. I flexed my arms, cracked my fingers, and prepared to
do stretching exercises. Suddenly I hesitated. I remembered it was time
for my weekly weigh-in. But when I stepped on the scale I could almost
hear it scream, "Owwwwwwwww!" It was time for a drastic change.

The words of my wife, Dana, echoed through my mind, "Tom, I've
been telling you. It's either time to go on a diet or buy a license plate."
You may laugh, but I was starting to look and feel like a semi-truck.
For too long I had packed more than 315 pounds on my six-foot, two-
inch frame. During ten years of marriage I had gone over and under that
mark like a yo-yo. Most often I tipped to the "over" side. While Dana

7

kept encouraging me to lose the excess baggage, her words never registered.

After I started traveling regularly with the Power Team, I found the courage to change. Long-time friend and team founder John Jacobs didn't let friendship get in the way of telling me what I needed to hear. Because he cared for me, he got in my face and demanded change, for the sake of being on the team and the good of my family. Most importantly, he said, I would miss my destiny and would miss seeing souls accepting Christ as Savior, if I died prematurely of obesity.

As I ran the hotel stairs night after night, John would scream, "Would you give more to USC football (where I played nose guard) than you would Jesus Christ?" Those words made me flinch. He refused to let up. "You've got to lose the weight! You're good for at least two million more souls!" His message sank deep into my spirit. Through tough love he pushed me toward a deeper commitment. Finally, I responded. In a little over two months, through diet, exercise, and prayer (a ton of prayer) I dropped more than fifty pounds and three waist sizes.

Dana marveled at the change she saw developing right before her eyes. "He's eating like a model," she gushed several times to our oldest son. "I've been telling him and praying for him for ten years to lose weight. And now he's finally doing it." One time, with all the innocence and wisdom a five-year-old could muster, Stephen looked up and said, "Well, Mom, maybe he just needed to hear it from a man!"

What insight! When it comes to us men, sometimes we just receive messages better from other men. At meetings sponsored by Edwin Louis Cole's Christian Men's Network, signs are often posted: "For Men Only." There is a good reason. It has nothing to do with feelings of male superiority or discrimination. Whenever a woman enters the building, men tend to clam up. But when challenged and surrounded by other men facing similar obstacles and struggles, most display a spirit of openness and receptiveness to change. The message breaks through.

I've seen this personally. The gospel penetrated the heart of my friend Tony Fetchel because of our man-to-man talk. When we met he was the star pitcher on Cal State Fullerton's nationally ranked baseball team; everyone called him by his nickname, "Wild Thing." That came from his ninety-four-mile-an-hour fastball, which often sailed away in unexpected directions. It represented the perfect parallel to his fast-paced, out-of-control lifestyle.

A mutual friend arranged our meeting. She was concerned about the dark depression that settled over Tony when he injured his right elbow. Projected as a first-round draft pick his junior year of college, he now faced a future without baseball. Life appeared hopeless. The saddest thing was that he had once committed his life to Jesus. But while pursuing his dream of playing in the major leagues, his relationship with Christ grew cold.

He told me later that the night he knocked on our door he expected a tall, thin geek to answer. When a 300-pound-plus monster in a cutoff sweatshirt greeted him, he thought, *This guy can't be a minister. He looks like he belongs on the defensive line of the Green Bay Packers.* No wonder he had a strange look on his face as I sat down at the dining room table with a Bible in my paw.

Tony explained how depressed he was over the loss of his favorite sport. He had tried to dull the pain with partying, alcohol, and loose relationships with women, only to find they left him feeling worthless and even emptier. He had even considered suicide, he said. He reluctantly agreed to see me only because he respected the friend who urged him to come.

"You mean to tell me that your life doesn't hold more value than a baseball?" I asked. "Are you telling me that if you can't throw a little white sphere of leather then you're going to kill yourself? That's the stupidest thing I have ever heard."

He looked stunned. I pressed on.

"The problem is that you may have at one time called Jesus your Savior, but you haven't met Him as Lord. Tony, baseball is the real God of your life. It occupies all your thoughts and dreams. It's what you're living for. God calls that idolatry!"

"That was the first time in my life I heard anyone talk straight with me," he told me later. "I had heard great sermons that challenged me. But it was being called out of my sin and selfishness, a call into a destiny by a man, one-on-one, that changed me."

This is the plan of *Ultimate Warriors*. You're going to hear it straight—from a man's point of view. But more importantly, many of the words you read will come from the Ultimate Man, Christ Jesus. I pray you will keep your eyes focused and your minds opened. If you will follow His example, it will revolutionize your life.

God's Mandate to Men

The Lord's plan for the world has never changed, and men, you are part of His plan. Through His Word, He is declaring as He did thousands of years ago, "As I live, all the earth will be filled with the glory of the LORD" (Num. 14:21). Amazingly, in spite of the crime, war, murder, perversion and hatred that humanity has spread across the earth, God's heart still goes out to the people He created.

We can see His strategic blueprint for humankind through the parable of the ten servants who received money from their master, to invest as they saw fit until he returned (Luke 19:11–27). Jesus represents the nobleman who traveled to a distant nation to receive a kingdom and promised to return. When the master called to his servants (some translations use the word "slaves") and gave them coins, he said, "Do business with this until I come back" (v. 13).

The literal translation of that sentence is, "Occupy until I return." Jesus set the pattern nearly two thousand years ago. As ambassadors for Christ we are to carry on the Lord's business. He has sent us into enemy territory called the world, with its misguided, selfish, self-glorifying, self-serving, and self-seeking ways. In the midst of the chaos, corruption, and evil of this world's value system, we (the people of God) are to act as a foreign occupation force. We are to enforce the terms of His treaty, the Bible. This powerful challenge causes many to shrink in fear or retreat to the comfort of air-conditioned dens and escapist pleasures. But to the man of God, it's a commissioning to shake this world for Jesus Christ.

Jesus is calling men to do more than bunker down in our comfort zones. He is the Ultimate Warrior. To bear His name we must be like Him. He told His followers that His sustenance came from doing His Father's business. Too many Christians fall short of this goal. They treat

Christ as a self-help guru sent to relieve them of all pressures and to constantly bandage their wounds. Such Christians render little service and rarely spread the gospel. God didn't put us on this planet just to get us to heaven. He wants us to take the principles and patterns of heaven to earth.

Sadly, for too many, church has become everything except what God intended. It has become a nursery, multimedia entertainment outlet, recreational hall, and self-fulfillment oasis—everything except its original design as a service center! God designed the church to launch men into their destiny and export the gospel to the lost, to heal the sick, to feed the hungry, to help the poor, and to dispatch God's grace to the nations.

In the 1990s we are witnessing a revival of historic proportions among men. During this decade the number of Promise Keepers rallies and attendance has expanded exponentially each year. The crowds would be even higher except that many of the rallies sell out months in advance. Though this and other participants in the Christian men's movements represent an incredible phenomenon, they only mark the first stage of revival.

I compare it to my two sons splashing in the Pacific for the first time. They gurgled with glee as the ocean mist sprayed across their faces, their toes tingling in the mixture of sand and surf. Wonder filled their eyes. We have since had a daughter and I am glad to jump in beside all of them as they wade in the tides. Yet I know more awaits them as they mature and discover the thrill of riding the waves.

This is the crux of *Ultimate Warriors*: Life is more than just accepting Christ as Savior. Accepting Jesus into our hearts as Lord only brings us to square one. There is so much beyond this for the followers of Christ. We can thank God for providing a way to be saved from the torments of hell and to enjoy the pleasures of heaven. But when we accept His gift of grace and become His child, He gives each of us a divine purpose. We are not saved by good works, even though Ephesians 2:8–10 makes it clear that we are saved to do good works.

As soldiers sent by Jesus, we have a sense of duty and mission burning deep within our hearts. One of my goals in this book is to teach you how to develop the kind of strong faith that will enable you to answer

11

the call to be an ultimate warrior. As Ed Cole says, "Enthusiasm is an emotion. Optimism is an attitude. Faith is a substance."[1] I want to teach you how to use your faith to

- be a servant of your home and community,

- discover your unique destiny,

- enter today's cultural warfare as a leader who will make an impact for god's glory,

- be an example not a follower.

Every man has a part to play in God's work here. No matter who you are and what you do, God has given you a particular sphere of influence in which you can lead. This applies to all men, whether you issue commands from the corporate boardroom or push a broom in the basement. After all, the janitor on the lower level can reach people the president will never meet. If you bear the name *Christian*, others will be watching to see how you act and react in various situations. You may be the only living, breathing example of Christ they will ever see.

Strong Women

Though this book is aimed at men, I think men can learn from a pair of strong female examples. These women radiate Christ. Like Deborah (Judg. 4:1–9), Esther (Esther 4:14), Jael (Judg. 4:17–22), and Mary, the mother of Jesus (Luke 1:35–38), when the Spirit of the Lord comes upon them, watch out!

One strong example I know intimately. Dana is a powerful woman of God. (That's why I married her.) When we were just friends, I would chuckle when men tried pickup lines on her. Using the Word, she fended off their advances using the "sword of the Spirit" (Eph. 6:17) to send them away in repentance or shame. Dana was bold in her witness while attending California State University, Long Beach. Even though she was the reigning Miss California State, she would do open-air preaching to students passing by the school bookstore. "I wear a crown of jewels on my head on the weekend, but today I stand before you wearing a crown of righteousness."

One of those who not only heard but responded to the gospel message was a young man named David Soto. Fed up with his lukewarm Christian lifestyle, he thought, *Finally, someone's living what she is preaching.* It challenged him down to his socks to see such a bold woman of faith, and he repented for his sinful compromise. Not only did Dave begin to live a victorious walk for Christ, he became a campus evangelist himself. He now leads a dynamic church in Austin, Texas, that has a strong outreach to forty thousand students at the University of Texas.

Dana's vision extended beyond southern California. She wanted to reach the world. The year the Summer Olympics came to Los Angeles she auditioned to carry a plaque during the opening and closing ceremonies. Each plaque bore the name of a participating country. Officials selected Dana to lead a small central African country during the processional. Although way back in the pack, she was delighted at being chosen.

Dana saw an opportunity to do more than carry placards. The week before the games began she passed out tracts and Bibles, translated into their native tongue, to athletes from that nation. When the coordinator learned about it she yanked Dana from leadership duties, fearing Dana's evangelism would cause World War III, and reduced her responsibilities to menial chores. That didn't stop Dana. Through building friendships, she led one of the other plaque carriers to Christ. Her name was Maureen, and she later became Mrs. David Soto. (See how God works?)

Just before the closing ceremonies were to begin, the ceremonial coordinator appeared in the area where Dana was standing. "One of the other girls is injured!" she cried. "I need someone 5-foot-8 to take her place." A host of women frantically waved their hands and jumped as they vied to take her spot. Dana quietly raised her hand. The director looked around, pointed at her, and said, "I want this one." Dana's humble servant heart prevailed and won favor with the very one who kicked her out earlier.

When Dana reached her position, she was astonished. Once lost in the shuffle, now she had been selected to lead the way as a representative for Greece. The only thing Dana could say was, "The Lord is faithful." From that day forward her life changed. Not only did she see how God had honored her witness; she knew she could influence nations. She has since accompanied me on many international missions and influenced thousands. I have seen Japanese citizens grow wide-eyed as she performs her interpretive dance glorifying Jesus. Russians and Filipinos have burst into tears as Dana ministers.

Lakita Garth is another woman who doesn't have the title "pastor" or "evangelist" posted on an office door. But she has a powerful testimony. As a song girl at USC, she refused to drink alcohol and took a stand for virginity despite intense ridicule. "Yeah, I'm missing out on a lot," she told more than one girl. "I miss out on those hangovers. I miss out on those trips to the clinic to see which sexually-transmitted disease my boyfriend gave me. I miss out having my heart emotionally ripped up by failed relationships." But as so often happens, when other students had problems they sought out Lakita because of her stability.

When Lakita met Dana, she was immediately suspicious; Lakita had never seen anyone so full of faith. While she loved God, she still feared following Him. She had her plans mapped out, including law school, prestige, and a six-figure income. She hated it when Dana and I challenged her and told her she had to allow God to be Lord of her life. If He sent her in directions other than law school, she would have to listen and obey. Well, God did speak, and she responded. Since that time the Lord turned her life into an adventure as she stood up for the cause of Christ. Now Jesus is the Chief Architect of her dreams.

God led Lakita into the entertainment world, where she has led many entertainment and sports personalities to salvation. Lakita recently made a CD with her group D'Vine, and they will stand up for God no matter what the circumstances or the cost.

Once a record producer from Ohio asked them to fly there to cut a demo tape. When they saw the off-color lyrics he had chosen for them, they shook their heads: "We're not going to sing anything we can't sing before Jesus." Enraged, the producer spat a few choice words and told them he was going to send them home. "Send me home because I've turned down more offers than taken to honor Jesus Christ."

"But it's just a job," rebutted the producer.

Glaringly, Lakita shot back, "I can't be bought!" Lakita continued, "You can send us home but unless you repent and allow Jesus into your life, you'll go to hell."

She said it with such force and conviction that he followed through with his promise. Then he bought a ticket on the same flight so he could come to California and see what kind of church would disciple such godly warriors. Today that producer—Keith Robertson, nephew of basketball star Oscar Robertson—is a member of our church. His partner, Michael Sechrest, was also saved and both became powerful church leaders. Both men are now making an impact in the contemporary Christian music industry. Lakita was recently called to testify before the United States Senate on the subject of funding abstinance programs in our public schools. Thousands of lives will one day thank this warrior of faith for her obedience to God's call on her life.

Men, you have your work cut out to keep up with women like this!

Wise Stewards

One of the keys to leadership is recognizing that none of us owns anything. We are merely stewards of what God has given us. If you don't believe that, when is the last time someone in a casket took anything underground besides burial clothes? The Lord gives us the ability to produce and merit employment, earn an income, and sustain a family. We must use these talents to further His kingdom. Jesus paid for your eternal life with His life, a heavy price.

Whether you're in your twenties, thirties, forties, or beyond, you have obligations:

- If a businessman, teacher, lawyer, doctor, or mechanic, you are called to influence your peers and culture. To do this, you must have boldness.

- If a husband and father, you are called to guide, guard, and lead your family. This requires biblical wisdom.

- If single, God wants you to boldly stand for Him among your peers. You will only do that if you have fearless convictions based on righteousness and truth.

We are all called to ignite revival and reformation in our society. This requires commitment, self-sacrifice, and endurance. It helps to surround yourself with men of good character. Considering the challenge, are you ready for the ride? If you choose to join us, our goal is to produce real men who love Jesus with all their hearts, honor their wives and families, exert strong, biblical leadership for society, and establish a godly style of masculinity in our culture. Our hope is that we will see a new breed of man who avoids the self-glory, materialism, and humanism of the Information Age. Such ultimate warriors will know that the secret of greatness is found in servanthood and stewardship of the influence, graces, and talents God has alloted us.

Men Willing to Fight

In his book *The De-Valuing of America*, former U.S. Education Secretary William Bennett wrote, "The battle for culture refers to the struggle over the principles, sentiments, ideas and political attitudes that define the permissible and the impermissible, the acceptable and the unacceptable, the preferred and the disdained, in speech, expression, attitude, conduct and politics. This battle is about music, art, poetry, literature, television programming, and movies; the mode of expression and conversation, official and unofficial, that express who and what we are, what we believe, and how we believe."[2]

This battlefield demands mature Christian leaders, namely men who are not afraid to risk scorn and ridicule for standing up and speaking out in a society that has lost its sense of shame and glorifies what is bad while attacking what is good. We desperately need men who will resist the evil in this modern generation. From the very young to the very old, it is time to rise up!

If you doubt the times are serious, consider that even the *Wall Street Journal*—not exactly a bastion of Christian activism—has pointed out the value of the church to combat our growing social ills. "You don't need a computer printout to figure out that kids who do God are less likely to do drugs or turn to crime or get pregnant," it editorialized. "In the inner city, churches are often the only institutions that still work."[3]

Bennett chronicled the devastation in America in a revised, updated edition of his book. He compiled shocking statistics for 1995's "Index of Leading Cultural Indicators" that show our decline since 1960:

16

- a 560 percent increase in violent crime
- a 400 percent increase in illegitimate births
- a quadrupling of divorce
- a 200 percent increase in teen suicide
- a drop of nearly eighty points in the average SAT scores of high school students
- the tripling of the percentage of children living in single-parent homes (This makes it simple to trace one of the primary reasons for our spreading crime problem.)

Do you want to be like the Ultimate Warrior? In the words of the apostle Paul, we are to "proclaim Him, admonishing every man and teaching every man with all wisdom, that we may present every man complete in Christ" (Col. 1:28). The late Supreme Court Justice Oliver Wendell Holmes Jr. once said, "The place for a man who is complete in all powers is in the fight."[4] We are sounding the alarm: *get in the fight*. Quit being a spectator and enter the arena. In doing so, you may change the world!

This may sound like too fearsome of a challenge, but it's not. As you build your life on the principles found in God's Word, He will transform your character and mold you into a brave-hearted warrior. I know these principles work because I have watched other men use them. Nick Gough, a successful businessman for many years, later entered full-time ministry. An associate pastor of a church in Orange County, California, he believes the salvation message without an emphasis on destiny is a "ripoff." He says of his earlier days attending MorningStar International. that our church gave him a passion to reach the world: "I tell my kids that wherever they go, whatever they do, they've got to believe God to make an impact and take dominion for Christ."

If you gather nothing else from *Ultimate Warriors*, remember that the truth you acquire is the real measure of your power and it will propel you into the fullness of God's purposes. Whether it is the truth about your values, purpose in life, or theology, truth is power. Ed Cole once told me that truth is like a nuclear bomb: the tighter you can compress it, the more explosive it becomes. He counseled, "Tom, never give a sermon unless you can condense it into one thought or sentence. Then you will have something powerful." In the same light, never build a life without making a definite statement of purpose and passion. As many of his followers know, Cole built his men's ministry on the basis of one definitive statement, "Christlikeness and manhood are synonymous."

So it is with your life. Sum up your destiny with a mission statement. This book will help provide some parameters for seeking purpose in Christ. Our society cries out for leaders with the hope and insight to recover from our national ills. You don't need to pile up a myriad of data to grasp the problems facing us; just watch the evening news. From politics to religion to education, the arts, and culture, don't let these conditions alarm you. Romans 8:19 says, "For the anxious longing of the creation waits eagerly for the revealing of the sons of God."

Men of God, you have been created for such a time as this!

Summing Up

The goal of this book is that each of you will reach your leadership potential and become the man God has called you to be. The "Basic Training" principles after each chapter review some of the key points in that chapter. The "Gut Checks" are designed to help you get a better picture of the blueprints of His plan for your life. For maximum results, we recommend keeping a personal notebook of your answers to these questions and other impressions. They will serve as a memorial of encouragement and a guidepost to keep you on the right track. Let the journey begin!

Basic Training

- *Jesus is Lord of all or not at all.* A prerequisite of salvation is lordship. Christ can't be your Savior without being Lord over every area of your life.

- *Occupy until Jesus returns.* Every man has gifts, talents, and abilities. They are to be used for spreading God's Word and good works that glorify Him.

- *We are owners of nothing, stewards of everything.* Every man has a sphere of influence. We are to steward that influence in taking the gospel to every area of society.

- *Christlikeness and manhood are synonymous* according to Dr. Edwin Louis Cole. The measure of a man's value, worth, and impact all come from his relationship with Jesus Christ.

Gut Check

1. Is God challenging you to do something? Maybe starting daily Bible reading and prayer, losing weight or exercising? Ask the Holy Spirit to give you a plan of attack for each one.

2. Does God have a dream for you? Look up Psalm 139:14, 16; Jeremiah 29:11–14; Ephesians 5:8, 11; Psalm 37:3–4, 23. List some keys from these Scriptures about your destiny.

3. What is God's mandate for the world? Look up Numbers 14:21 and Luke 19:11–27. How does that relate to your destiny?

4. Look up Ephesians 2:8–10. Why do you think God gave us the ability to be born again?

5. List some areas of morality that are under assault in your community. What can you do? Write a plan of action.

6. If you are a mature believer, ask God to identify men you can mentor through friendship and Bible study. Ask Him to also bring you mature men who can disciple you.

2

SPECTATORS
VERSUS PARTICIPANTS

You don't learn to hold your own in the world by standing on guard
but by attacking and getting well-hammered yourself.
—George Bernard Shaw

Though decades of use have aged its concrete bones, the Los Angeles Coliseum is still a majestic stadium. Home to titanic college and professional football clashes and several runnings of the Summer Olympics, it radiates history and tradition. As a college student, I watched two teams slugging it out on the muddy turf to determine who would go to the Rose Bowl. Walking in the gate that afternoon, I didn't know that USC would not only win the game but become that season's national champion.

The atmosphere in the Coliseum captured my imagination. If you never have stood in the midst of eighty thousand frenzied fans, you can't understand the electricity. The offensive lines that then outweighed the Dallas Cowboys was an awesome sight, as was the Trojan mascot stepping the sidelines on his white horse, poised to circle the track after each USC touchdown.

Though soaked to the bone by a driving rainstorm, I sat and marveled at one of the greatest, most forceful teams in modern college football history. Yet, before the second half, other feelings stirred inside. Watching this spectacle stirred feelings of dissatisfaction with being a passive spectator. I wanted to run on the field and become part of this prestigious team. A hope burned within that I could join the famous "Trojan family." I wanted to do something, anything, to contribute to USC's success. I didn't care if I only carried the water buckets. (Some claim I didn't do much more.)

I had just been accepted at the university. I knew that if I didn't go for it at that time I would never have another chance. If you will permit me to steal a line from the movie *Rudy*, I was tired of people telling me what I could not do. Throughout my life teachers, coaches, and friends repeated negative messages. It was time to take a chance, get out of the stands, and step into battle.

A ticket to a game may cost twenty-five to fifty dollars, or even more—expensive admission to become an armchair quarterback. But cost does not begin to match the price paid by the competitors on the field. Time, sweat, blood, and broken bones are just some of the dues in the football fraternity. I sustained eight broken noses during my playing days.

But the fear of a busted beak didn't compare to the fear of my first meeting with defensive line coach Marv Goux (pronounced goo), a former USC player and one of its best mentors. At that team meeting Goux jumped in my face, scaring me half to death and barking, "Sirotnak, I want to see what you're made of because you're going to learn to love to hit or die. Ha, ha, ha." That day I determined I would be a participant, if I didn't die first. It reminds me of an advertisement for an athletic shoe featuring San Diego Charger linebacker Junior Seau. In it he is wearing a USC workout shirt that reads, "The shirt you can buy, but the glory is earned."

It took a tough initiation to earn a spot at USC. I'll never forget the afternoon I noticed coaches setting up for the dive drill. The drill matched offensive and defensive linemen one-on-one. The blocker tried to open a hole for the tailback, who had to dart between a pair of cones about four yards apart. Not expecting to see action, I leaned back on my heels to watch. Suddenly Goux barked, "Sirotnak!"

As I stumbled onto the field I was so nervous, my jersey looked like I had been sitting in another rainstorm. I crouched in position, and then looked up and gulped. Twice. Future all-pro running back Marcus Allen would carry the ball. Blocking for him: future all-pro lineman Keith Van Horn. Looking back I now jokingly kid, "He looked big enough to eat hay and dumb enough to enjoy it." The forearms on this six-foot-six, 280-pound hulk looked like Christmas hams. I sighed, "God, just get me through this drill."

They snapped the ball. Somehow I bucked under Van Horn's shoulder pads and got some leverage. I threw him down to the inside, sealing off the gap. When Allen reached me I buried my helmet in his chest, earning my first broken nose. Dreaming of stardom for stopping our star runner, I was so intent on smacking him I forget to wrap him up with my arms. Allen busted my tackle and swiveled down the field, leaving me in a sweaty, dusty pile of humiliation.

The coaches enjoyed a good belly-laugh as they chortled, "Welcome to the big leagues." Though I thought of quitting, I quickly vowed to myself that they would have to kill me or kick me off the team before I ever quit. My experience provided excellent training for the tougher struggles I would face in life. Like Rudy, I never achieved football stardom, yet I earned the honor of being team captain for one game my senior year against Washington State. I only got in for one play, but it was worth it. My satisfaction came from more than running on the field. On the inside I learned about

- being a champion (champions are not those who never fail, but those who never quit),
- the benefits of setting high goals,
- upholding standards of excellence,
- the blessing of sacrificing your own interests for the betterment of others—a team spirit,
- the power of camaraderie as men build one another up to help one another succeed.

Living for Christ

When I became a Christian I saw how the lessons of football applied to a walk with Christ. Once I had tasted the thrill of the playing field at the Coliseum, I was ruined for merely sitting in the stands. I wanted to see action. Likewise, in my relationship with Jesus, I couldn't just talk about faith; I had to live it. I saw that many choose to sit back in a church pew and never take action, just constantly finding fault and criticizing others. I vowed to get on the front lines of battle and spread the gospel. As a Christian, I wanted to know the Bible so I could carry its truth into action. I wanted a piece of the devil, and I wanted to take back what he stole from the people of God!

Lyman Beecher (1775–1863) was one of the great preachers in the early days of our nation. President of Lane Theological Seminary, he was the father of Harriet Beecher Stowe. The ideas forcefully described in her novel, *Uncle Tom's Cabin,* became a driving force in the abolition of slavery. Commenting on his life, Beecher said, "I was made for action. The Lord drove me, but I was ready. I have always been going at full speed . . . harnessed to the chariot of Christ, whose wheels of fire have rolled onward, high and dreadful to His foes and glorious to his friends."[1]

Are you harnessed to Christ? Are you living out your good ideas or God's ideas for your life? Is the Lord the author and architect of your dreams? Or are you? Worse yet, do you fail to see how God has orchestrated you into His symphony? The most important question is: are you a man of talk or action? Man of God, it is time to decide to live a life of impact for Jesus.

DeNail Sparks is an outstanding example of a man who has the burning desire to live for Christ. He didn't choose an easy mission field when he took over leadership of a ministry at the University of Nevada at Reno. The city's name may conjure up visions of entertainment and good times, but its gambling, alcoholism, prostitution, and other misguided practices have ruined countless lives, marriages, and homes.

A few years ago this former USC defensive tackle couldn't claim any destiny or purpose. He was an angry, hostile man who used football to appease his violent, inner turmoil. He wasn't just spiritually lost. De-Nail lived on the edge of disaster, enmeshed in an underground ring of drug trafficking, violence, and crime. He didn't come to Los Angeles hoping for an NFL career. He wanted to expand his drug ring and recruit teammates as distributors. He couldn't imagine living past age twenty-two. Why should he? Few of his friends and associates had survived that long.

The night he came to a chapel service as a freshman, six-foot-four, 270-pound "Big D" had the stare of death in his eyes. That night he heard that God had a plan for each person; no matter how messed up or rotten life might seem, the Lord could change it. I told him that sin would always promise to serve and please but would actually only enslave and dominate his life and lead to death. But God had a plan to give him abundant life. This word of destiny struck a chord in DeNail's heart. He repented, made Jesus Lord of his life, and soon was baptized.

"All hell broke loose that night," he says. "The hell of confusion, anger, fear, and hopelessness broke off my life for the first time. When Jesus changed my nature, I became a new man with a new life ahead of me. I didn't want to sit in the same pew in the same church all my life without doing something for God. I had to decide whether I was going to be a 'home boy' (as his friends would say) or a forerunner for Christ. Was I willing to pay the price?"

He was. A few years later at another meeting, I asked if he was ready to lead the fledgling ministry in Reno that I had helped organize. His eyes grew wide at my challenge to enter full-time service. Yet, he knew the Lord was calling him to higher ground, to become a missionary to his own people and nation. DeNail and his wife, LeNair, have since seen many students sparked by the call of God's destiny.

"Most Christians are too satisfied with the knowledge that they have obtained salvation," he says. "But they don't ask God what their mission is while they're on this planet. It's easy to talk about doing something for the Lord, but when He speaks you have to put up or shut up. When we received the call to ministry we had to step out of the boat. It caused us to lean on Him even more. We learned the rock under us is solid."

As long as we remain on earth, the body of Christ needs rock-solid believers willing to fulfill the Great Commission, which refers to Jesus' command found in Matthew 28:18–20 (and other New Testament passages) to go into the world, find converts, baptize them, and make them His disciples, who in turn will subdue nations by the teachings of Jesus Christ. *Webster's 1828 Dictionary*—the best biblically-based source for a word search—defines commission as: "Any writing from proper authority, given to a person as his warrant (authorization) for exercising certain powers or the performance of his duty."

Jesus established His authority when He rose from His grave. He is the only One to die on the cross for mankind and the only One to overcome death. The word *authority* comes from the Greek word *exousia*, which means "power divinely given, authority to act." Jesus said in Matthew 28 that all power has been given to Him, so He is commissioning us as His ambassadors to go with that power and teach the nations obedience to His gospel.

As you discover your destiny and begin to make an impact in your sphere of influence, you become a participant in God's plan. This means *each of you* plays a role, whether you live in the sprawling metropolis of New York City or a small town on the Midwestern plains. Two-thirds of the name *God* is G-O! Going is the process of evangelism, whose goal is to make disciples of Christ.

When I first went out as an evangelist, God promised He would never place me in circumstances from which there was no escape. But He didn't promise it would be easy. Since then I have been kicked, almost lit on fire, cursed, and spit on; I have ducked rocks, apples, oranges, and other projectiles thrown my way. But these and other harassments haven't caused me to lose heart. The abuse is nothing compared to seeing men and women changed through Christ. As 2 Corinthians 4:8–10 says, "We are afflicted in every way, but not crushed; . . . persecuted, but not forsaken; . . . always carrying about in the body the dying of Jesus, that the life of Jesus also may be manifested in our body." There is a price tag to being a participant.

Evangelists at Work

Some of the mightiest evangelism occurs in the daily marketplace—under an oil pan at the automotive service center; over lunch in the office cafeteria; in the locker room after a game of pickup basketball; or on the golf course, when someone in your foursome asks why you don't burst into rage over a bad slice.

Paul spelled out this truth to Timothy in 2 Timothy 4:5: "But you, be sober in all things, endure hardship, do the work of an evangelist, fulfill your ministry." No matter what your occupation, your most important calling is to be an evangelist in your community. Some Christians struggle with this concept because too many churches have become a one-man show. The pastor performs and the audience watches. Pastors are vital to our mission, but the body of Christ is made up of many leaders at all levels of society.

The apostle Paul didn't make his living from preaching. He was a tradesman, making tents (Acts 18:3). That is the source of the term tentmaker, someone who spreads the gospel but doesn't depend on missions support or a pastoral salary. One of the best tentmakers I know is Charlie Coons, who came to the Lord while attending a seminar exposing the dark side of modern-day rock-and-roll music.

Growing up in Hawaii, Charlie developed a tender spot in his heart for Russia. He and his grandmother mailed hundreds of Christmas cards to Soviet Christians who were persecuted by the Communist government. Still, because of a lack of discipleship, his commitment to Christ grew cold. Instead, He pursued playing rock music and acting in stage plays. In college, addictions to drugs, alcohol, and sex swept him further away from God. That changed the night one of the seminar leaders confronted him. "You may know Jesus as Savior," he said, "but I doubt it. He can't be your Savior unless He is in first place in every area of your life. That means He must be Lord." That night Charlie experienced a change of nature from a sinner to a child of God!

Charlie soon had an opportunity to act on his long-standing concern for Russia through joining a small mission support team. The timing was all wrong. He had two more semesters of school and his old lifestyle had left him heavily in debt. But after he prayed, counseled with other Christians, and felt deep peace in his heart, he decided to go.

During three years in Russia he saw how God provided for his needs. His group found a home in three days and enjoyed daily meals even though they often didn't know where the food would come from. The biggest miracle occurred when Charlie applied for a job at the American Embassy. Despite the steep odds against him obtaining employment, he became the food service and catering manager.

God had more in store. Besides orchestrating press conferences, receptions, and congressional dinners, the embassy hosted one reception for former president Richard Nixon, two for President Bill Clinton, and one for Vice-president Al Gore. During these visits Charlie had an opportunity to give copies of Ed Cole's books, *Maximized Manhood* and *Strong Men in Tough Times*, to our nation's top officials. Charlie told President Clinton, "Mr. President, I'm praying that you would ask God to show you where you are wrong and have the courage to change it. And, that you would ask God to show you where you are right and have the wisdom to increase it. God is not mute if we are not deaf."

Wow! Could you be ready at a moment's notice to witness to world leaders? In that brief moment, Charlie couldn't pray with the president, but he sowed good seed with the opportunity he had. If you set your desires on learning God's Word and His principles so you can teach them to others, the Holy Spirit will help you perfect your gifts, talents, and witnessing ability. Then you will have a proven ministry, and God will arrange divine appointments for you, just as He did for Charlie Coons.

No matter what your occupation or profession, you are to serve as a minister to expand the Lord's kingdom. God wants His men in every walk of life. If you're an auto mechanic, think of your witness through doing quality work for fair rates. People will take notice and often open a window of opportunity for a Christian witness. The same goes for plumbers, painters, doctors, lawyers, professors, writers, actors, and politicians. This calls for aggressive activists, not passive, apathetic pew-sitters. We need more men of zeal and passion to see Jesus exalted in the marketplace, church, home, and society.

Two prevailing attitudes inhibit the carrying out of Jesus' Great Commission:

- *Men who think it's someone else's job.* They are content with giving a small donation and letting someone else do the work, someone such as a pastor, missionary, or evangelist.

27

- *Men who moan, "I don't have time."* God's work is never convenient. If there is no time, why do men always find time for baseball, football, basketball, golf, fishing, movies, concerts, picnics, vacations, school plays, bowling, and television?

To show you the seriousness of the need for more workers to spread the gospel, look at these statistics from a 1993 study of the status of Christianity around the world.

- Christians as a percentage of the world: 33.5%.

- Affiliated church members: 1.72 billion.

- Practicing Christians: 1.26 billion.

- Great Commission (active) Christians: 616 million.[2]

As you can see, Great Commission Christians make up slightly more than one-third of church members. They are participants. The rest are spectators. Participants choose battles of endurance, persecution, and mockery from the world's elite. Instead of taking the path of least resistance or bowing to political pressures, they arm themselves with God's Word. They stand on His principles and lay down their lives, reputations, and wealth for Christ. They are ready to turn the world right side up.

Active Christians are the kind of leaders people will follow. You can be such a man if you yield to Jesus' direction in every area of your life. Jesus won't be your Lord until you give Him control of your life, your job, your family, and your future. Giving God control means dying to *your* wants, *your* needs, *your* feelings, and *your* cravings. What God wants, thinks, and feels is of utmost importance. Ed Cole stresses, "God's power is released to the degree of our obedience to Him."[3]

Giving God control may sound easy, but putting it into daily practice is much tougher. Countless Christians who once were in the battle are now on the sidelines, nursing their wounds, carrying grudges, or worn out from fatigue, usually because they tried to fight it in their own strength. Apathy and compromise can easily touch any of us. Jesus said it happens through the "worries of the world and deceitfulness of riches and the temporary pleasures of this life" (Luke 8:14). We must constantly keep up our guard to ward off such attacks. We must stay in the game.

Suit Up and Play

One of my favorite verses is Philippians 1:6, where Paul wrote, "For I am confident of this very thing, that He who began a good work in you will perfect it until the day of Christ Jesus." Those are comforting and encouraging words, but don't overlook the previous verse, where Paul mentions "your participation in the gospel." In other words, as God is perfecting His good work in you, He also wants you to suit up and get into the game.

As Christians, we often place too much stock in appearances: how many people came to a rally or meeting, how many walked forward to accept Christ, or how many were baptized. Instead, our emphasis should be on how many disciples we train for Christ. This is a long-term process that is not easily measured. This calls for a two-fold strategy:

1. *Awaken and activate passive, apathetic Christians into full-time service.* Second Corinthians 5:20 says, "Therefore, we are ambassadors for Christ, as though God were entreating through us; we beg you on behalf of Christ, be reconciled to God."

2. *Convert the unsaved into followers of Christ and establish them in the foundations of faith, producing disciples (see Gal. 2:20).* Our motto: "Every Christian is a leader for the cause." Our philosophy: "Win them, train them, send them."

One of the great myths about Christianity is that it requires a quiet, shy, pacifistic outlook. That does not square with the Bible's instructions. Peter writes in 1 Peter 1:13, "Therefore, gird your minds for action." In Ephesians 6:11–14, Paul commands us to "put on the full armor of God," "stand firm," and "resist in the evil day." Elsewhere he tells us to "be alert" (1 Thess. 5:6) and "fight the good fight" (1 Tim. 6:12).

Man of God, this means you! God didn't give you the armor listed in Ephesians 6:13–17 so you could sit on the bench and snooze. He wants you to go to war and fight for the cause of Christ and to establish

His kingdom on the earth. When He left, He promised to return. He doesn't expect you to go to sleep while He's gone. If you wouldn't do that at the job where you earn a salary, why would you consider it in matters of eternal significance?

Are you man enough to step into the spiritual arena? You may be a big talker at Christian meetings, but do you wilt when others mock you and sneer at your faith? Are you ready to pick up the sword of God's Word and fight with that weapon? Are you willing to put your reputation and image aside so you can leave a mark in the sands of time? If you are tired of lukewarm, minor league Christianity and want to enter the majors, the world awaits your influence.

One of my favorite stories about a man of action wanting to leave a legacy is about Walt Jones of Tacoma, Washington, a feisty, quick-witted, 104-year-old man with a zest for life.

His story follows:

> Walt outlived his third wife, to whom he was married for fifty-two years. When she died, someone said to Walt that it must be sad losing such a long-time friend. His response was, "Well, of course it was, but then again it may be for the best. She kind of petered out on me in the last decade."
>
> Walt went on to explain that he wanted to purchase a motor home to visit all forty-eight of the contiguous states ten years earlier, when he was ninety-four. His wife wouldn't hear of it, using excuses that, at his age, he would get them killed, they would fall victims to violent crime, or they would die and there wouldn't be a funeral parlor around. Walt persisted, "I'd like to make footprints in the sands of time before I check out. But you can't make footprints in the sands of time if you're sitting on your butt . . . unless you want to make butt prints in the sands of time.[4]

Men, are you with me? I don't want to be among those namby-pamby Christians without a purpose or definitive calling. Or one of the lukewarm pew-sitters who only show up for church when they want to be entertained. I definitely don't want to go down as a couch potato in the annals of history. The world needs participants, bold men of stature equipped to conquer their world for Christ. The world needs men who will get off their backsides and be willing to cause a holy revolt.

Do you want to be a trained, armed, and dangerous member of God's army? First you need to know the importance of your destiny, so read on.

Basic Training

- *You'll never make an impact without causing a collision.* Your witness shines brightest in the sparks of confrontation (see 2 Tim. 3:12; John 15:20).

- *Without a cause worth dying for, life has little meaning.* Read about the relentless courage of the men of God in Daniel 3:12–30.

- *God is obliged to complete what He begins.* Destiny is God-designed, not self-ordained. Get about God's business and He will get about yours (Matt. 6:33).

- *Don't be intimidated by the devil.* If Satan doesn't start something with you, start something with him.

- *When the men of God rise up to rule, society is blessed.* See Proverbs 29:2.

- *God's power is released in our lives according to the degree of our obedience to Him.*

Gut Check

1. Are you harnessed to Jesus Christ? What are your goals and dreams? Write them down. Are they God-ordained or self-initiated?

2. Read Hebrews 11:8–10. When Abraham was called out of the midst of familiar surroundings, who designed his future dreams, plans, and goals? How does this affect your outlook?

3. A vital part of Abraham's destiny rested in his having an heir, which was seemingly impossible because of his advanced age (Heb. 11:11). God wants to bring you, too, into a destiny that may look impossible. Read Hebrews 11:1–6 and write out how you will achieve your maximum potential for God.

4. Evaluate your calling. Are you on course? Are you answering God's call or just building bigger barns and accumulating things? If you

are not sure of the Lord's call, pray and ask Him to open your eyes. Leave space in your notebook to record ideas as God reveals them.

5. What price did Moses pay to deliver his generation? (See Heb. 11:24–26). What price are you willing to pay?

6. Evaluate your heart honestly. Have you been driven by manmade goals or selfish ambitions? If so, let them die. Ask God to resurrect new dreams so you will be useful for His glory. As you pray, write down what He brings to your mind.

3

A DATE
WITH DESTINY

Sow a thought and you reap an act;
Sow an act and you reap a habit;
Sow a habit and you reap a character;
Sow a character and you reap a destiny.

—D. James Kennedy

I t was a Saturday, early in January of 1986. Butterflies fluttered in my stomach. Excitement and tension filled the air. Grabbing some isolated moments of sleep during a restless night, I awoke in the early dawn hours. No, it wasn't time for the Rose Bowl. Or the Super Bowl. This was much bigger. Today was the Marriage Bowl.

I had waited so long for that special woman, my perfect partner. Contemplating the incredible series of seemingly minor events that brought us together, a deep sense of God's presence overwhelmed me. As we sought God and His righteousness long before we dreamed of marriage, He saw fit to meld two unique individuals into one. That day truly represented the Master's plan.

More than marriage put chills in my spine. This day showed me that the Lord felt deep concern about everything that happened in my life, and that if I allowed Him to guide my steps, I could fulfill my God-given potential and achieve my destiny. This holds true for each disciple of Jesus Christ. Psalm 37:23 says, "The steps of a man are established by the LORD; and He delights in his way."

Years later, our son Stephen watched our wedding video with wide-eyed wonder. Dana ended the ceremony by saying, "To all of our future children, I just want to say hi and we love you." I jumped in to add, "Stephen Rice" (named after the man who led me to faith in Christ); Dana said, "Sharon Rose"; and in unison we closed, "Tommy Jr." As an afterthought, I looked soberly into the camera and said with parental authority, "And go clean up your room."

Years later, we are batting three-for-three. More important, we have seen the fulfillment of Psalm 139:16, "Thine eyes have seen my unformed substance; and in Thy book they were all written, the days that were ordained for me, when as yet there was not one of them." In watching this video, Stephen discovered that God had a plan and purpose for him. The Lord even called Stephen by name years before his birth. What a wonderful impression to leave on a young boy. Stephen knows he is not an accident of chance but a special creation of God for a holy purpose.

This is a vital concept. Too many people mistakenly believe they are a product of chance, an accident of conception or an unwanted pregnancy. But it is almighty God who opens up the womb. When God initiates something as wonderful as you, it isn't an accident. You are valuable and loved by God. If you will follow Him, He will give your life meaning, provide redemption, and establish your destiny.

Long ago God spoke to a young man named Jeremiah and confirmed his destiny with the words, "'Before I formed you in the womb I knew you; and before you were born I consecrated you; I have appointed you as a prophet to the nations'" (Jer. 1:5). I believe the God of Jeremiah is still calling men to act as His spokesmen to a lost generation throughout the world.

God challenges modern men to believe in divine destiny, plunder and pillage the devil's domain, and establish His kingdom. As Paul encouraged Timothy, "Join with me in suffering for the gospel according to the power of God, who has saved us, and called us with a holy calling, not according to our works, but according to His own purpose and grace which was granted us in Christ Jesus from all eternity" (2 Tim. 1:8–9).

Paying the Price

Destiny! It sounds so glamorous but few will carry through and pay the price that comes with it. Look at some notable biblical failures:

Judas. Greed disqualified him from royal service. He walked next to the Son of God, but a thieving heart led him to betray Him for a trifling sum of money. Overcome with remorse, Judas then turned his back on the available forgiveness and hanged himself. What a sad end for someone who missed his destiny. (Matt. 27:3–5)

King Saul. He lost his crown because of pride and fear of other men. Commanded by God to destroy Amalek, he folded under pressure and let greedy underlings save some spoils. That marked the beginning of the end. Saul later became consumed with jealousy of David when he saw the young shepherd had the heart for God he lacked. Saul ultimately died in disgrace. (1 Sam. 15:9–11)

Samson. Samson became a judge of Israel. His great strength and victories won over the Philistines and earned him biblical tributes. But I believe he fell short of maximizing his full potential because of his continuing problem with lust. He may have conquered the enemy, but he was disgraced by allowing ungodly women to lead him astray. He fell short of God's best. (Judges 16:20)

Esau. Esau forfeited his opportunity to be part of Christ's royal lineage by treating his birthright casually. Selling out for momentary pleasure and gratification—not even tears of remorse and repentance could regain this treasure (Gen. 25:27–34). Though designed to be great, Esau became forever branded immoral and godless. (Heb. 12:16–17).

Why is paying the price so important? Isn't it enough to accept Christ as Savior and gain a ticket to heaven? Not if you want to establish His kingdom on earth. I'm convinced what scares the devil to death is someone causing trouble for him right now. People of destiny are people of impact, spelling disaster for the rulers of darkness.

Nor has Satan come up with any new tricks. His quickest, easiest method to ruining a man's destiny is through sin. First John 2:16 warns, "For all that is in the world, the lust of the flesh and the lust of the eyes and the boastful pride of life, is not from the Father, but is from the world." If there is anything unclean or that you have not surrendered to God, get rid of it. Pray that God would remove the stumbling blocks and give you access to your destiny. When we have entanglements with sin in our lives, it will only produce dysfunctional destinies.

Answering My Call

I remember when I felt God's destiny tugging at my heart. I was experiencing what the Bible had said all along, "Sin was pleasureable for a season." Until my senior year of college, I lived by my own desires and impulses. But partying with football teammates and fraternity brothers became a "burnout." So did dreams of earning a marketing degree and financial prosperity. Once I turned over my life to Jesus, I knew that full-time ministry was my calling.

As Rice Broocks—the man who led me to Christ—discipled me, it seemed as if he were pulling destiny out of me. I had long felt called to be a leader, but fear and insecurity caused those feelings to lay dormant. With the eye of a visionary, Rice stressed how changing America's college campuses could literally change the world. He talked about raising up an army of Christian leaders who would one day fill key positions in our society.

"If our God is the only hope for the nation, then God's people must be trained by biblical reasoning in every area of life," he said. The more he talked about revival and biblical restoration of our nation, the more I wanted to play a part. One day he told me if I could stay on the right path for two more months, he would take me wherever he was going. Soon we were flying east to the University of Virginia. My new friend and NFL Hall of Famer, Rosey Grier, was part of our group. I remember the campus newspaper mocking his bold faith, sneering, "Take back Rosey, we've had our fill, let him sell beer if he's over the hill."

That was the first time I felt righteous anger. I wanted to retaliate but was so green I wasn't sure what to do. So I went to the place where

I felt the most comfortable: the gym. I didn't know how to present the plan of salvation but I could lift weights. Loading up the bar with 450 pounds, I bench pressed the massive weight, grunting to add a little drama. Setting it down, I watched the awe in people's faces. Then I lifted it a few more times.

Finally, I said, "Hey, if you think that's impressive, you should hear this guy named Rice speak tonight. It will change your life." That night about twenty-five men from the gym came to our meeting. Ten got saved, of which four wound up in full-time ministry. That incident ignited the spark of destiny that still consumes me today—to tell people about Jesus.

However, you don't find your destiny through casual effort. It took great, godly men to draw it out of me, and it likely will be that way for you. That is why it is so important to be associated with godly men who are determined to answer God's call and make disciples. You need the encouragement and vision that others can impart to you as they strive to fulfill their destiny.

I was fortunate to have many men providing me wisdom and guidance as a young Christian, especially my pastor Phil Bonasso. He set up my first public testimony at a church in Long Beach; another new believer came with us. Afterward we went out for some spicy Mexican food, but it was Phil's heart for discipleship that really burned. He bluntly told us how goofy we had looked up on stage that night.

"Tom, when you stand up before a group as a man of God, command their attention," he said, thrusting his finger next to my nose. "Stick your chest out and speak boldly. Don't stammer, 'Golly, gee, it's sure good to be saved' with your hands stuck down in your pockets. And stop speaking like a girl with that squeaky little voice. If you're going to be a disciple, you have to present the gospel with confidence. Be a man!"

That may sound harsh, but it was what I needed to hear. Phil believed we had a destiny. He wanted us to walk with a godly stature and dignity as men who would one day help change the world. The best advice he gave us was this foundational principle: "You won't win any battles apart from the Bible. You have to plant the seeds of the Word in your heart so they can grow and bring you into the knowledge of your calling and destiny. As you read God's Word, He can speak to you and use it to bring divine revelation into your spirit."

I could fill this book with the names of many servants of God who have trained leaders across the nation and the world. But my purpose is not to glorify men. My point is that God helps strengthen you through other believers. We must realize that a wealth of strength and maturity can be drawn from those who have gone ahead of us. It is critical to find men where you live who can break the bread of life (God's Word) with you and instill in you the vision, courage, and purpose to pursue your destiny.

Carrying On

Once a man has a revelation of his destiny, and the inspiration of the Holy Spirit to fulfill that destiny, he will be unshakable. It will be next to impossible to deter him, lure him away, or bribe him away from his calling. The man who is governed by a God-given destiny will develop an attack mentality; he goes on the offensive. On the other hand, a man who lacks vision tends to be ruled by momentary emotions, feelings, and circumstances. Destiny is not a matter of developing a superior strategy, intellect, or talent. What matters is whether a man will seize destiny's opportunities as God opens the doors.

As an example to us I believe that even the Lord Jesus had to fight for His destiny and purpose. Significantly, His first test immediately followed confirmation of His ministry by the heavenly Father: "Now it came about when all the people were baptized, that Jesus also was baptized, and while He was praying, heaven was opened, and the Holy Spirit descended upon Him in bodily form like a dove, and a voice came out of heaven, 'Thou art My beloved Son, in Thee I am well-pleased'" (Luke 3:21–22).

Soon after, He confronted Satan in the wilderness (read Luke 4:1–14). His battle was much greater than overcoming the flesh. The devil didn't really care whether Jesus could turn stones into bread, if He changed His heavenly allegiance, or whether He foolishly threw Himself off the pinnacle of the temple. Satan attacked Christ by challenging His destiny. The devil preceded each of three temptations with, "If you are the Son of

God . . . ." The enemy tried to cast doubt on Christ's identity, character, and purpose.

Instead, Christ withstood the test. His victory set the foundation for His ministry. Can you see the personal parallels? Satan will test you, often through wilderness experiences, trying to cast doubt on your calling and purpose. For example, not everyone is called to full-time professional ministry. But if you believe that is God's will, you can be assured Satan will test you. He will toss seeds of doubt into your mind, spurring you on to wonder, "Am I really supposed to do that? Wouldn't I be more useful to the ministry as a successful businessman? What about my family responsibilities?"

The devil tests Christians in other occupations too. He will whisper lies like, "You don't have to be that committed. After all, people will be turned off by some fanatic. Lighten up a little bit. . . . C'mon, you don't need to give so much money to that missions project. Make it up next year when you're more financially secure. . . . Try this little short cut; nobody will know about it."

But deception and compromise won't work on a man who knows his position in Christ. If he has paid the price to be in fellowship with his Creator, then God's power will produce unshakable world changers. First John 5:4–5 reassures, "For whatever is born of God overcomes the world; and this is the victory that has overcome the world—our faith. And who is the one who overcomes the world, but he who believes that Jesus is the Son of God?" Strong faith in God along with intense perseverance will cause you to fulfill your destiny. You must depend on that for your entire life. I do, and I'm not special. If He could take a bumbling, stuttering, shy, insecure nobody like me, He can inspire you to greatness—and empower you to reach it.

As a new convert, I zealously met with God, spending up to two hours a day in Bible study and prayer. One morning as I sat by my bed, I had a vision that I was running. As I ran, I picked up countries and tucked them under my arms. Finally, I stood at God's throne and laid the countries at the Lord's feet. As I meditated further, God communicated with my spirit, telling me I would be a worldwide evangelist and bring healing to the nations. He said I would help bring revival and see miracles occur in thousands of lives.

Such a magnificent calling struck me with awe. I was too shy to tell anyone and immediately doubted this experience. *Can it be true?* I thought. *Maybe it was just my imagination.* However, the following week a respected pastor encouraged me with a similar message: "Tom, God has called you to the world as a revivalist. You are going to see miracles as people come to get saved." That was all I needed to hear. That day I met the Jesus of my destiny. I have never doubted it again.

My destiny became non-negotiable. The passing pleasures of the world and other temptations suddenly held no attraction. I remember the night Rice Broocks drove me back to my fraternity house after a meeting. We pulled up to the raucous noises of an *Animal House*-type of party. As a fresh convert, Rice felt like he was throwing me into a lion's den. I know because he delayed dropping me off, circling the three-block stretch of fraternity row a dozen times. As he drove he elaborated on Christ's lordship and His plan for my life.

When I walked inside, I had set my resolve. I ignored the music, passed up the keg of beer, and headed straight for my room. I thought I had passed the test. But when I opened the door, I saw a gorgeous sorority sister lying in my bed. Talk about a moment of decision! Shaking, I remembered Rice's words and my salvation experience. Yes, this was an incredible temptation. Yes, I had waited a lifetime for something like this to happen. But conviction shot through me. What I did behind closed doors did matter. If I fell now, it would only be a matter of time before others learned about it. And, it would be easier to repeat the mistake.

No, I vowed, I would not return to my old ways. Breathing deeply, I said, "Hey, listen, I've become a Christian. I've made a decision that my life is going to be different from now on. I just can't do it." A look of shock crossed her face. Finally, she said, "Well, if that's what you want to do, I understand," and meekly left.

Afterward, I sat alone in my room, stunned. In twenty-two years nothing like this had ever happened. But as soon as I dedicated my life to Christ, a Bathsheba (2 Sam. 11:1–5) appears on my doorstep? With such an obvious temptation, I realized the devil had used her as bait to lure me away from God. Deep down inside, I knew the Lord had some awesome plans in mind if I remained faithful. Thank God that His grace carries us when we don't feel too strong.

Keys to Destiny

1. A man of destiny is a man of power! Notice what happened after Jesus resisted Satan's temptations in the wilderness. Luke 4:14 says, "And Jesus returned to Galilee in the power of the Spirit." Later, verse 32 picks up, "And they [the people] were amazed at His teaching, for His message was with authority." These verses show how power comes upon a man who knows his destiny.

Recognizing our calling in Christ ignites fervor in the heart of man. He must enter the war between good and evil. The man of destiny burns with determination to even the score with God's enemies. His righteous indignation and love for God won't allow him to stand still. Despite twists and turns, he clings to his destiny as if he were riding the world's largest roller coaster. And that is always best when you're right up front.

2. A man of destiny knows the importance of lordship. This means he gives God first place in his life. Period. Trying to achieve your destiny without the lordship of Jesus is comparable to launching a rocket with a teacup of water. Like the spaceship, you won't get too far. Destiny is synonymous with lordship. You must be in the right posture before God can reveal your destiny. Lordship reminds the wise disciple of who is orchestrating and steering the events of his life. Through His guidance and power we achieve His ultimate goals. The fact that God can accomplish His plans through limited, fallible people demonstrates His awesome power. In our quest for destiny we must be preoccupied with trusting and obeying God and following His will with our whole heart.

3. A man of destiny dreams big dreams. We serve a huge God. He wants to remove the limits we often place on ourselves and focus on the all-powerful Jesus who lives inside of us. God is looking for men with the kind of faith that will rely on His strength to carry the day. Look at the tests of Moses and Gideon. Moses led an enslaved nation to freedom without bombs, tanks, or bullets. Gideon marched his puny-sized army of three hundred up against thousands of Midianites.

To put God's instructions into modern-day language, He said, "Look, guys, I know your shortcomings, fears, and insecurities, but I'm not talking about you. I'm talking about the Lord who created you and will move on your behalf." These men's weaknesses didn't limit God and neither will yours. God is far greater than any weakness you may see! As 1 Corinthians 1:27 says, "God has chosen the foolish things of the world to shame the wise, and God has chosen the weak things of the world to shame the things which are strong."

4. *A man of destiny uses his faith.* God is looking for men who will dare to seize opportunities. Abraham was such a man. God prophesied to him that his descendants would be the heirs of the world because of his faith (Rom. 4:13). When Abraham was old and yet childless, God spoke his destiny into existence (Rom. 4:17). This painted a vivid picture of the future. Abraham remained obedient to the vision that God gave him.

If he looked at the circumstances, particularly his advanced age, there is no way Abraham could have believed that God would give him a son. But Romans 4:20–21 says, "Yet, with respect to the promise of God, he did not waver in unbelief, but grew strong in faith, giving glory to God, and being fully assured that what He had promised, He was able also to perform." Abraham followed a simple but effective formula to his destiny:

- He received God's Word as a guaranteed promise (Gen. 17:1–9).
- He refused to doubt (James 1:5–8).
- He grew strong in faith (Rom. 10:17).
- He praised God in advance (1 Cor. 15:57; Ps. 100:4–5).
- He received the reward (2 Tim. 4:7–8; James 1:12).

5. *A man of destiny doesn't procrastinate.* The devil loves to hear you groan, "Oh, I'll do it tomorrow." When God calls you to do something, you need to act. Respond when Christ speaks; delaying is a sure path to failure. Don't you dare wait for more favorable circumstances, until you feel ready or are more comfortable and secure. Many fear knowing God's destiny because they then would be responsible to act. Or, they are afraid it will ruin their plans and dreams. The longer you wait to respond to God's call, the more limited will be your impact. Procrastination and poor choices will cause you to live below the level of life that God has planned for you.

The longer you wait to seize your destiny the more limited your options. Take a man who waits until he turns forty-five to train for the

Olympics. By then he is restricted to sports like target shooting, archery, or yachting. Don't waste your destiny, especially if you are a young man. God doesn't intend youth to be a playground of harmful experimentation and fulfilling lustful passions. He wants you to attack the devil's domain and boldly stand on the front lines of the nation's cultural war. Has God given you a dream? Then go for it!

6. *A man of destiny will flourish in the local church.* In Matthew 16:18 Jesus said the gates of hell would not overpower His church. If He thinks that highly of church, how do you think you should value it? A church will protect and perfect the children of destiny (Eph. 2:19–22; 1 Cor. 12:12–18; Eph. 4:11–16). God wants His church to triumph over the gates of hell in every city. Therefore, He gives each of us a role to play in a local church. You can't expect an army assignment for one. God doesn't endorse spiritual Lone Rangers in His kingdom.

God made a covenant with His people setting us into a family of believers known as the church. As we sit under that covering, our destinies are protected from the forces of hell. The church is not just a safe haven for believers. According to Ephesians 4:11–16, it is also meant to equip the saints so they can drive the forces of hell backward and incorporate God's kingdom on the earth.

I question any man who claims he can fulfill his destiny apart from the local church. Through preaching the Word and setting standards, the church gives boundaries to my destiny—not to limit me but to keep me on track. Submitting to church authority keeps me from turning my life into a disaster. As a young Christian, my pastor told me three critical choices shaped my destiny: (1) my decision to serve God, (2) who I married, and (3) what church I joined. All are related to family, whether God's or my own. Just as we revere our immediate family, we should love our church home. It provides proper credibility, authority, accountability to enhance my goals, and calling.

Use It or Lose It

God frowns on the lazy, stagnant, and slothful. You are either building His kingdom or tearing it down. Today you must determine whether you will be an active participant in spreading the gospel of

Christ around the world, or a clogged artery hindering the flow of God's Word to a dying world. God doesn't treat idleness or half-hearted efforts lightly. Proverbs 18:9 warns, "He also who is slack in his work is brother to him who destroys."

Some of you need to get fed up with the devil oppressing and bullying you. Through God's Word and prayer we must call on our heavenly Father to kick Satan out of the events of your life and invite Jesus to direct them as your Lord. The Bible compares Satan to a roaring lion, looking for someone to devour (1 Pet. 5:8). Those lions roam throughout all nations, prowling through cities and seeking to destroy homes.

There is only way to deal with the lions in our land—kill them. Don't be like the cowardly sluggard who can only wail with dismay, "'There is a lion in the road! A lion is in the open square!'" (Prov. 26:13). The sons of destiny who follow Jesus, the Lion of the Tribe of Judah, will slay Satan's beasts by refusing to retreat from them (Prov. 30:30). Will you fight for your God-given destiny? Read on to learn more about a basic requirement: servanthood.

Basic Training

- *Destiny is a choice, not a matter of chance.* You can choose to follow your path—divine or deadly. Choose wisely!

- *You are not an accident of creation.* See Psalm 139:13–16, 2 Timothy 1:9; Romans 8:28–31; Ephesians 1:5, 11.

- *Your destiny is non-negotiable.* Remember the story of the beginning of Jesus' ministry in Luke 4:1–30.

- *Destiny flourishes under the covering of the local church.* The church at Antioch confirmed Paul and Barnabas' callings (Acts 13:1–3; Eph. 3:10–12).

- *Your destiny will not go beyond the confines of prayer.* Prayer and intimacy with God remove the limits from a man's destiny (Phil. 4:13; John 5:19–20).

Gut Check

1. If you are single, have you asked God to lead you in seeking a mate? How do you expect your future partner to help you fulfill your destiny?

2. If you are married, how does your mate help you achieve your destiny? Have you told her?

3. Have you defined your destiny? If not, have you asked others for their spiritual insights into your character?

4. What are you doing to reach your destiny? Write out your personal mission statement of who you are and what you have been called to do. Memorize it!

5. If you didn't read it earlier, look at Luke 4:1–14. What tests has the devil sent you lately? Considering Jesus' example, what is the best way to fight the enemy when he tempts you?

6. What goals and dreams has God given you?

4

THE WAY UP
IS DOWN

God did not save you to be a sensation; He saved you to be a servant.
—*Anonymous*

I f you think greatness comes from sitting on a platform and accepting accolades from the adoring masses, think again. Read the following story of an American officer from the Revolutionary War who sent some of his men to construct a badly needed bridge:

There were not nearly enough men and work was getting on very slowly. Up rode a commanding-looking man and spoke to the officer in charge, who was urging on his men but doing nothing himself.

"You haven't enough men for the job, have you?"

"No, Sir. We need some help."

"Why don't you lend a hand yourself?" asked the man on horseback.

"Me, Sir? Why, I am a corporal," replied the officer, rather affronted at the suggestion.

"Ah, true," quietly replied the other, and getting off his horse he labored with the men until the job was done. Then he mounted again, and as he rode off he said to the officer, "Corporal, the next time you have a job to put through and too few men to do it you had better send for the Commander-in-Chief, and I will come again." It was General (George) Washington.[1]

Servanthood is not short-term apprenticeship training. It is the badge of the lifelong follower of Christ. When John the Baptist announced the coming of Jesus, he warned the hypocritical Pharisees, "Therefore bring forth fruit in keeping with repentance" (Matt. 3:8). He was telling these religious leaders to turn from their arrogant, high-handed rulership and imitate the servanthood of the coming Master.

None of us will ever be so brilliant or successful that we will be relieved of our duty to serve our brothers and sisters in Christ. Another word for *servant* is *minister*. As His ambassadors we are all ministers. Clergy and laity don't toil on different levels or serve separate kingdoms. For too long we have divided pastors and leaders, such as elders and deacons, from the rest of the church. Everyone is called to evangelize, fast, and pray.

Likewise, there are not two codes of conduct. It is not OK for you to sip on a six-pack of beer but wrong for the pastor. As ministers, regardless of vocation, we stand equal before God. He expects us all to pursue righteousness. Servants should courageously strive for the highest standard of conduct, not settle for the lowest common denominator.

Heaven Isn't for Hirelings

Hireling. An unfamiliar word? A synonym is *mercenary*, someone who works solely for monetary gain or personal advantage. Hirelings have no feelings for the people they serve because they are only interested in results, such as riches, security, or acclaim. Their impure motives don't come from the love of Christ. Jesus rebuked the status-seeking Pharisees with this question, "How can you believe, when you receive glory from one another, and you do not seek the glory that is from the one and only God?" (John 5:44).

Such religiously-pious hirelings are still alive and active. These "spiritual pimps" (participants in the gospel for personal gain) will be disqualified from their spiritual inheritance. You probably know a few hirelings—men who sit in the pew on Sundays for the sake of appearance. They won't tithe or give of their time. They won't make any personal sacrifices or tolerate persecution and aren't eager to face any trials. The hireling's existence revolves around, "What's in it for me?"

Jesus pointed out ministers driven by selfish motives in John 10:12–13, "He who is a hireling, and not a shepherd, who is not the owner of the sheep, beholds the wolf coming, and leaves the sheep, and flees, and the wolf snatches them, and scatters them. He flees because he is a hireling, and is not concerned about the sheep." Hirelings love their wages more than their work. They want the promises of God but none of the responsibilities.

The follower of Christ expresses concern about the Lord's work and how best to please Him first instead of self. Those who render service to God as worship and adoration will receive heavenly rewards and His approval. The Lord will say, "Well done, good and faithful slave; . . . enter into the joy of your master" (Matt. 25:21).

Don't be misled by the use of the word *slave* in Matthew 25. It is often translated *bondservant*. I look at the distinction this way: Bondservants willingly serve God because they believe in servanthood, but a man with a slave mentality follows Christ grudgingly. He is bound up by legalism, obeying God out of fear of His wrath and eternal punishment. The slave gives the bare minimum he thinks he must to look good, please fellow church members, or chalk up spiritual brownie points. Did you ever hear someone say, "We don't *have to go* to church in the middle of the week because we went on Sunday"? People who go because they *have to* instead of *want to* will get more from staying home. At least at home they can relax.

While slaves see only a burden to service, the sons of God concentrate on the blessings and privileges of sacrifice. They willingly serve Him because they know the truth of Jesus' words, "For My yoke is easy, and My load is light" (Matt. 11:30). For them, the difference in serving God is one of attitude. Our son Stephen can turn a menial task like dumping the trash in the garbage can—a whopping thirty-foot journey—into a venture more difficult than parting the Red Sea. Lips trembling, face cringing, and body slumped over, he looks as if I had shackled him with a ball and chain. But if I say, "Hey, buddy, as soon as you throw away the trash we're heading out for ice cream," he turns into Superman. His perspective changed, the task represents pleasurable service because of the sweet reward.

When a man is born again into God's kingdom, he understands and appreciates how Jesus saved him from the vicious consequences of hell. This perspective moves him to service. As believers, we are children of God and should care more about what our Father wants than our desires. Jesus promised, "If anyone serves Me, let him follow Me; and where I am, there shall My servant also be; if any one serves Me, the Father will honor him" (John 12:26).

However, serving God is no guarantee of smooth sailing. Do not expect the world to applaud you for going against the grain of self-serving, self-glorifying, self-fulfilling philosophies. The Lord's ways are thoroughly opposed to the world's. That is why some of the great principles of faith sound like paradoxes straight out of George Orwell's classic novel, *1984*:

- To gain your life, you must first lose it.

- To be strong, you must first admit your weakness.

- To get, you must first give.

- To be exalted, you must first be humble.

- The last shall be first.

- Then there is the great truth that forms the focus of this chapter: whoever wishes to be great must be the servant of all.

We can't claim the lordship of Jesus as if it were a free ticket to heaven or a badge of superiority. Above all, His Lordship means servanthood. This is why we should consider ourselves as owning nothing. We are merely stewards of God's gifts and creation. Yet, so many people want to get puffed up over things they did nothing to gain, or that in large measure depended on others' love and generosity:

- the color of their skin,

- the size of their bank account,

- the greatness of their talents,

- the beauty of their looks (now there's a real accident of birth),

- the ability to advance in their career.

There is nothing wrong with a healthy self-esteem about your accomplishments, but don't mistakenly think you arrived at your station in life solely on your own merits. You didn't give birth to yourself, change your diapers in infancy, teach yourself in school, or feed yourself as a child. As an adult you can't function on the job or in society without others' assistance and cooperation. You have no reason for boasting. For it is "not that we are adequate in ourselves to consider anything as coming from ourselves, but our adequacy is from God, who also made us adequate as servants of a new covenant" (2 Cor. 3:5–6).

The Servant's Heart

As a servant you need to pray to your heavenly Father and ask Him questions like: How do You want me to steward my income? How should I treat my body? How can I better shepherd my wife and children? What career path do You want me to follow? How can I best influence my local community? What impact can I make on a national scale? As servants, God expects us to grow spiritually, mature in all ways, and increase our responsibilities. If we don't produce, He counts us among the worthless, lazy, and unbelieving (Luke 19:13–22 and 1 Tim. 5:8).

The world cannot understand the freedom and fulfillment that service produces in a man's heart. Servanthood defies the conventional wisdom of this culture. Modern, New Age philosophies have spread like wildfire because of their self-centered approach. The crux of their teachings is that each person is the center of his or her universe and thus deserves pampering and self-indulgence. No wonder so many advertisements proclaim, "You deserve it!" and senior citizens' bumper stickers brag, "I'm spending my children's inheritance!" That may be a joke, but the attitude behind it is no laughing matter. Persons should be more concerned with what they leave behind than what they consume.

Our modern social climate is producing the chilling result of a world filled with cold-hearted souls. The commonplace acceptance of abortion is one example of a selfish, uncaring world. A child is a gift from God and a divine opportunity to shape the future. Yet, many look on a fetus as an inconvenience, something to be done away with until a "better" time. The seeds of hard-heartedness sown through abortion have sprouted new fruit: those eager to rid society of the handicapped and elderly via assisted suicide and other forms of euthanasia.

This is why unselfish service presents such a strong witness. Christ's light shines powerfully in the midst of great darkness. As a servant you represent the character of Jesus' name. You are His example of truth, grace, and righteousness to the world. Don't dishonor His name by your actions. The lack of a servant-like heart is a primary root of lukewarm Christianity. I believe the Holy Spirit sheds great tears over the lack of service by those who profess allegiance to His name.

This is nothing new. Thousands of years ago the Spirit of the Lord asked Malachi, "A son honors his father, and a servant his master. Then if I am father, where is My honor? And if I am a master, where is My respect?" (Mal. 1:6). The people in Malachi's day wanted God's favor but would not render the service or the money owed to Him. Instead, they wanted to give Him their leftovers.

The same occurs now. Have you ever seen football players kneel in the back of the end zone after a touchdown? I know some whose Christian service begins and ends with that pious act. They pay homage with heavenly high-fives, but afterward they resume lifestyles that fail to glorify God. I know how that goes on because before I served the Lord I used to give Him this kind of lip service.

God doesn't want your leftover sacrifices of convenience. You cannot give to God only what you think you can afford to lose. He wants your best, from the home front to the offering plate and the neighborhood to the workplace. No compromise. No self-interest. Just pure Christlike service. We didn't come into this life to make big headlines. We were created as joint heirs and colaborers with Christ, who is the Ultimate Servant. Through His character of service, Jesus proved to be the greatest man to ever live. He came as an envoy to help the desolate and distressed. A loving servant to those afflicted by disease and oppression. He pressed on relentlessly, often denying Himself food and rest to follow these noble goals. After a lifetime of preparation He laid down His life to reconcile sinful humans to God and gain us direct access to His throne. Jesus died to rescue me—and you. What a servant! What love!

This is why you will never find satisfaction in making a big name for yourself, building a personal empire, earning a fortune, and gaining tributes for your personal fortitude or praise for your ingenuity. Significance doesn't come from preeminence among men. Meaning in life is only found in Christ by dying to self and living as His servant.

A scholar once told me that the majority of persons who enter the history books are not even aware of their roles during their lifetimes. This characterizes the contribution by the majority of our nation's founding fathers. They weren't looking for a fight with their motherland. The majority were God-fearing citizens defending their consciences from heavy-handed British intervention. They sacrificed to secure the liberties and freedoms we often take for granted. They had a willingness to stake all they owned for the cause of liberty. For example, of the fifty-six signers of the Declaration of Independence, nearly half either died in the Revolutionary War, were captured by the British, or had their homes burned, looted, or defaced. These patriots sacrificed life, family, and reputation to render service for our benefit.

No Crown without the Cross

Jesus spelled out the paragon of greatness when addressing His disciples: "'Among the heathen, kings are tyrants and each minor official lords it over those beneath him. But among you it is quite different. Anyone wanting to be a leader among you must be your servant. And if you want to be right at the top, you must serve like a slave. Your attitude must be like my own, for I, the Messiah, did not come to be served, but to serve, and to give my life as a ransom for many'" (Matt. 20:25–28, TLB).

To set the scene, James and John were hiding behind their mother's skirt. Afraid to pose the question themselves, they got her to ask the Lord if they could have a high position of honor in heaven. One wanted to sit on His right, the other on the left. When the remaining ten disciples heard about their request, they became indignant. (If that doesn't convince you that Christ's disciples were the same kind of common, ordinary people alive today, nothing will.)

James and John asked the wrong question. They were acting as if the battle had already been fought, the victory won, and the spoils ready to be claimed. Instead of laboring in His kingdom, they automatically wanted the honors and glory that followed. When they should have asked for the grace to lift their cross, they were running after the splendor of their crowns.

Likewise, it is easy for us to fall into the same trap, wanting glory but leaving labor and suffering to someone else. In today's self-seeking world it seems everyone wants to be the commander-in-chief when what Jesus needs is an army of servants. Besides, you can't be the chief cornerstone of God's kingdom; Isaiah 28:16 states that title already belongs to the Prince of Peace.

Why shouldn't you be striving for self-glory? Look at James and John. Jesus unmasks the folly and ambition of their request by reminding them of the suffering and discipline that await every follower of Christ. Suffering is as much a part of joining with the Lord as baptism and Communion. I don't necessarily mean physical pain or the kind of harsh oppression Christ faced when He went to the cross. But turning over our rights to serve God is laborious, costly, and, at times, very difficult.

- "Behold, I have refined you, but not as silver; I have tested you in the furnace of affliction" (Isa. 48:10).

- "And I shall bring you into the wilderness of the peoples, and there I shall enter into judgment with you face to face" (Ezek. 20:35).

- "For to you it has been granted for Christ's sake, not only to believe in Him, but also to suffer for His sake" (Phil. 1:29).

- "Suffer hardship with me as a good soldier of Christ Jesus" (2 Tim. 2:3).

Just as James and John needed the gentle reminder the Lord provided, so do all who aspire to Christian service. We don't join the body of Christ for popularity, status, plaudits, or promotions. Christianity is not a means to become puffed up with pompous piety. It means losing our identity and fame so that we can devote our energies to lifting up the Lord.

As the twenty-first century approaches, the world is seeking to throw off every shred of moral restraint. Men, while our generation and its culture rushes madly toward destruction, you must take stock of yourself and see whether you have the stuff to be champions for Christ. Count the cost of dying to self and resolve in your heart that no request will be too great in the King's service. The crowns of Christ are reserved for those who by modesty, self-denial, and service are prepared for them. The keys to greatness come from humility, diligence, and purity in our service to God.

We can see these qualities at work in Jesus. Nowhere did He better prove His willingness to serve than by washing the disciples' feet (read John 13:1–17). The awesomeness of His example comes shining through when you remember the place and era in which this occurred. Washing someone's feet sounds humbling enough. But what about after the person wore sandals all day and tramped through a dry, dusty land? Even more significant is the disdain society had for servants of the ancient Mediterranean culture; they were the lowest of the low.

For a man who called Himself King to stoop to the most unpretentious, humble position imaginable shocked His disciples. Imagine yourself in that position, being served by a man you had watched open blind eyes, cast out demons, heal the sick, and confront the hypocritical Pharisees with such wisdom they quit asking him questions.

When you consider this kind of humility in action, displays of domineering, controlling, or arrogant attitudes (including your own) ought to put a stench in your nostrils and be considered repulsive.

Real-Life Servant

Servanthood is not just a lesson buried in the history books or confined to flowery-sounding motivational speeches. It works. No better example exists than a friend of mine who pastors a church in Southern California. Gary and his wife, Gina, have experienced astounding miracles since 1987, when they moved to the city where they now live. He believes the wave of God they are seeing there may soon move across the nation.

Gary and I spent time together last winter at a meeting sponsored by the Christian Men's Network. My eyes widened when he told me about driving up in a limousine that shuttled about a dozen city officials and other civic leaders to the event. Gary offered to pay their way because he wanted them to hear Ed Cole's teaching about destiny and character. Gary hoped Dr. Cole's teachings would rub off on his hometown civic leaders and that they would implement those biblical principles in governing their local affairs. That day, some of the city's top officials responded to the call of God.

He also described exciting things that God is doing in their city, from bringing gang members to Christ to taking the gospel into schools to prayer meetings with the mayor and city manager. It all began with a message Gary and Gina received in prayer after they felt led to move there: if they would serve their city, not for political motives or pastoral power, then God would literally give them an opportunity to influence local government.

The first area where Gary put that into effect was in the local ministerial alliance; in the past he had never been affiliated with this kind of organization. As Gary crossed denominational lines to work closely with other pastors, God opened doors. After Gary became president, government agencies began calling the alliance to ask for help. Among them were school officials who wanted to include the story of Christ's birth, death, and resurrection as historical fact in junior high textbooks, and needed advice on appropriate resources. The district also invited pastors to participate in an annual faculty conference on how to better teach sexual abstinence to students.

In addition, school officials invited an ex-gang member to speak at more than a dozen junior high and high schools about staying off drugs. Though he couldn't make a direct gospel presentation, when responding to questions he shared how faith gave him the will to avoid drugs. He also attracted more than 1,500 students to an evening gospel-based rally. The area's leading gangs attended the meeting, held the same night violence erupted in Los Angeles after the Rodney King verdicts. Despite ominous warnings of riots spreading there, the city remained peaceful.

"I don't understand about Jesus, but I've never seen gangs sit together and listen," the amazed police chief told Gary later. "Whatever you're doing, keep it up." Later, the department invited Gina to become the first female police chaplain in their region. Her position includes an opportunity to write a newspaper column, and in 1995 she was named "Woman of the Year" by police, probation officers, and social service workers.

But the most amazing thing Gary and Gina witnessed came after their city was teetering on the brink of bankruptcy. Gary believes the Christians' faithful prayers led to the election of a mayor and various council members who are born-again Christians. A new city manager is also a believer, and when the old police chief stepped down, a Christian took his place.

Early in 1996 Gary and his wife began holding twice-a-month prayer meetings with the mayor and city manager. Gary described the moving scene that occurred the first time they sought divine direction: "I asked the mayor to pray and he said, 'God, I'm tired of having good ideas. I need God ideas for this city. Give me Your wisdom and Your understanding of how to implement Your plans into this city.'"

Those words moved Gary and Gina to tears. When they looked up, the city manager was also weeping. After they finished, the city manager said, "What's taking place here right now—"

"Is history," Gary interrupted.

"Right," the city manager agreed. "In a real sense, we're going back and regaining the fundamental principles that caused our nation to be great. I'm a historian myself. Initially in our nation there was protection for the church. The voice of God came through the church. Government was to be there, following and serving the people rather than separating church and state. The church was to be the moral fiber that held our individual rights and this nation's Constitution together. The protection, provided under the Bill of Rights was so the government couldn't come in and manipulate or control church. We feel strongly that what we're coming back into is that government is poised to serve, not to lead, in this city. God has called the church to hear His voice and vision and we are here to serve you."

Sound incredible? In the first chapter we discussed God's command to occupy until He returns. As Gary and Gina served their city, they saw how the Lord provides His children the ability to carry out that directive. When we serve we are fit to rule. After we are subject to ultimate authority we can be trusted to use it wisely. Continue on to read more about the qualifications of a servant and what it takes to be a great leader.

Basic Training

- *You are not saved to be a sensation but a servant* (Matt. 20:25–28).

- *Never require something from those working with or under you that you would not do yourself.*

- *Heaven is not for hirelings.* We serve out of love for Christ and desire to be obedient to His will (Matt. 25:21).

- *Unselfish service breeds uncommon results.* In a world of cold hearts and self-serving schemes, coming in the opposite spirit ushers in the presence of God's grace.

Gut Check

1. See Ephesians 2:1–10. How are you an ambassador for Christ? Is there something else you could be doing?

2. What is your mission? See Ephesians 5:8–14 and 2 Peter 2:9. (What is your service to God to produce?)

3. Who is the Great Commission addressed to and what are its chief commands? See Matthew 28:18–20 and Matthew 24:14.

4. Can you think of any areas of society that need the influence of God's Word? What can you do to make that happen?

5. How does God's command to make disciples affect you? Name three areas where the Lord has given you influence.

6. What does Matthew 16:19 say? Can you think of areas in your city, school district, political arenas, and cultural institutions where the gates of hell need to fall? List them and begin to fight through prayer, fasting, and civic action.

7. List ways you can serve in the local church.

5

LEADERSHIP'S BRAND LABEL

You are only qualified to lead to the degree you are willing to serve.
—*Edwin Louis Cole*

The former USC fraternity house that our ministry had leased for a campus center resembled the local dump. Shattered windows dotted the outside. Paint peeled off the frame and shutters. The inside walls looked worse, undoubtedly trashed during the previous occupants' wild parties. After surveying the first floor, I shuddered to think what lay below. I had drawn the assignment of cleaning the basement.

Slowly descending the stairs, I shook my head as my eyes adjusted to the dim light. It was a pit of perversion. Gleaming forth from jet black walls were fluorescent slogans of death like, "Charles Manson's Here" and "Kill." Surrounding them were a bevy of *Playboy* and *Penthouse* centerfolds. Wrinkling my nose at the foul, musty odor, goose bumps ran up and down my arms as I set a trash can in place and picked up a paint brush.

However, on the outside our church administrator, Robert Atkinson, was getting ready to tackle a tougher job. Atop the sloped roof of the three-story house the frat boys had painted a huge beer logo. That was not the kind of image we wanted to portray on a Christian outpost, so Robert vowed to paint it over. He grabbed the biggest ladder he could find, yet even with an extension pole couldn't quite reach the roof.

After awhile in the basement I needed some fresh air and came upstairs to survey our crew's progress. Seeing Robert's dilemma, I spotted two super-sized, sturdy office desks donated to us by the university and lugged them over to him. Stacking them on top of each other and setting some heavy objects at the ladder's base, I steadied it while he climbed. When he reached the top I yelled up, "Ya OK, buddy?" He yelled back, "Yeah, Champ, doing great."

After watching him paint for a moment, I decided he could manage on his own and went to chat with some guys working on the other side of the house. Five or ten minutes later a blood-curdling scream sounded: "Whoaaahhh! Whoaaahhh! Aahhhhhhhh!" followed by a huge "crash!" We raced around the house to find Robert lying flat on his back, clinging to the top rungs of the ladder. Somehow it had slipped from its moorings and wedged between the desks and the house before bending in half—away from the house.

"Man are you OK?" we shouted. We looked him over like doctors, gingerly searching for cuts, bruises, blood, or broken bones. After realizing his only injuries were some minor scrapes and a wounded ego, we burst into hysterical laughter.

"How could I have let you talk me into such a stupid idea?" Robert said recently as we reminisced about the incident.

"It may have been stupid," I grinned. "But I didn't go up the ladder."

Not only did he recover from the blows to his pride, before the afternoon ended Robert had blotted out the beer sign too. Robert is not only our administrator/handyman but also is one of our key pastors lending spiritual guidance to many. Every ministry needs its Robert Atkinsons. Men and women who take on the dirty jobs and are willing to stand in the shadows are as important as any minister on the front lines. The body of Christ isn't about superstars, but lifting up *the* Superstar, Christ Jesus.

Servanthood is the way you become a leader in God's army, not through human cunning, worldly wisdom, feats of strength, political alliances, or influential pressure groups. Spiritual leadership is not a position to campaign for like political office. It comes through His call and others' recognition of God working in your life and takes place in His timing. Embracing servanthood means striving for its three leading qualities that qualify men to be leaders: humility, diligence, and purity.

Humility

Whatever a man's occupational and spiritual roles, the essential quality for serving God is a humble heart. All great Christian men possess this integral character trait. The Bible says never again has a man lived like Moses, "whom the LORD knew face to face" (Deut. 34:10). Want to have a hot line to heaven like Moses? Remember his brand label—humility. Numbers 12:3 says, "Now the man Moses was very humble, more than any man who was on the face of the earth."

Though Moses was born in very humble surroundings, through circumstances he rose to occupy a high place in Egypt's palaces. But he lost his royal status after being forced to flee the country; while defending a fellow Hebrew he killed an Egyptian. Stripped of pride and self-sufficiency, he spent forty years in the wilderness, where he tended sheep for his father-in-law, Jethro. Broken of any sense of superiority, presumption, and conceit, he became fit for the Lord's use. The biblical pattern comes from Proverbs 18:12, "Humility goes before honor."

Humility has played a role in other famous men's lives.

One of the premier pioneers in the scientific community, Isaac Newton (1642–1727), had a deep faith in Christ. The world often sings the praises of this mathematician, scientist, and philosopher. He discovered the law of gravity, formulated the three laws of motion, helped develop calculus into a comprehensive branch of mathematics, and constructed the first reflecting telescope. All these great discoveries originated with Newton's spiritual beliefs:

"I find more sure marks of authenticity in the Bible than in any profane history whatsoever," he once said. "There is one God, the Father, ever living, omnipresent, omniscient, almighty, the Maker of heaven and earth, and one Mediator between God and man, the man Jesus Christ."[1] This premise was at the base of everything he discovered. It should not be a surprise that the Lord revealed to Newton so many properties of the earth He created. First Peter 5:5 says, "God is opposed to the proud, but gives grace to the humble."

As a young man I discovered the need for humility when pride led me into a dead end by my senior year of college. The thrill of football would soon end, the goal of a USC business degree didn't seem that wonderful any more, and a close relationship with a special woman had just crumbled due to my lack of character. God designed this desert period to break me so He could mold me into a useful servant. When I humbled myself before Jesus Christ and surrendered to Him, I began to understand His awesome plan for my life. True riches and honor, which the world cannot understand nor imitate, only come from serving God and walking humbly in His destiny. Proverbs 22:4 says, "The reward of humility and the fear of the LORD are riches, honor and life."

After the Lord rescued me from my insane empty lifestyle I felt Him calling me to share His Word. Rather than serving as a pastor, though, I felt His leading to become an evangelist. That excited me! A pointless existence fueled by liquor and low self-esteem faded away, replaced by a sense of purpose and value. Revitalized, I envisioned preaching to multitudes around the world and seeing thousands flood to the altars for prayers of repentance. I wanted to lead others down the path of peace and fulfillment that I had found.

Pulsing with energy, I went to share this good news with my pastor. Bursting into his office, I grinned, "Pastor Phil, the Lord's called me to be an evangelist and I'm ready to go." Instead of jumping up to dance a jig, he looked back with a deadpan gaze and fiddled with his glasses. After what seemed to be an eternity, he replied, "Now, isn't that just wonderful? Here is your first assignment."

I could hardly wait. My heart raced as I awaited his directions. Where would I go? In what kind of vast arena would I speak? Who would be there waiting to hear my message? How many of them would accept Jesus as their Savior?

"Boy, go out and get a job."

His words felt like a punch from Mike Tyson that left me gasping for air. Blood drained from my face. My knees quivered.

"Tom, don't be too upset," he soothed. "Some areas of your character need work. You need to be faithful to serve in the church while you're earning a living doing something else. Prove yourself up to the challenge and the time will pass quickly."

We sometimes treat God's servants with a casual attitude. I had sashayed into Phil's office with an air of familiarity, puffed up with youthful zeal. What I needed was admonishment from my mentor to count the cost. In delivering that message, he acted as the Lord's ambassador and gave me fatherly guidance. The Almighty knew exactly what He was doing. I needed to be humbled to show me who was in charge. When I applied for a summer job at a fast-food restaurant, I felt like I might sink into the floor tiles. My buddies were headed to jobs with IBM, investment firms, or regional sales offices. Meanwhile, my destiny consisted of scrubbing toilets, unloading supply trucks, and wrestling roast beef.

Pastor Phil knew how I felt. He had been there. It is the same course every noble man of God follows. He kept encouraging me with a phrase based on Matthew 25:23, "Faithful in little, faithful in much." Those words set the tone for my attitude. I determined that I was working for the Lord, not the restaurant. So I served my manager and customers with joy, working as unto the Lord. Soon I found I loved my job, even when I had to get up at 5:00 A.M. to slide sides of raw meat into the oven.

No, I wouldn't want to go back to those days. I have been called to other tasks. But this was a precious time in my Christian walk. I met with God, rose to a challenge, and let Jesus mold my character. I never dreamed that less than a year later I would become a campus evangelist at my alma mater; or that I would rise to a ministry leadership role. Or, eventually, that God would lead me around the world with internationally acclaimed ministries such as John Jacob's Power Team, Greg Ball's Champions for Christ, and the Christian Men's Network with Dr. Edwin Louis Cole.

Today I stand on stage and break massive stacks of bricks with a crushing blow from my elbow, rip apart telephone books, smash ten-foot-thick blocks of ice, and run through piles of two-by-fours. Huge crowds at Power Team crusades often squeal words of encouragement, egged on by John Jacobs shouting, "Help him! Help the Cannonball (my nickname on the team)! C'mon Big Tommy, c'mon! You can do it!" Frequently Dr. Cole and I will be doing "our thing" in front of thousands of men, encouraging them that Christlikeness and manhood are synonymous.

At other times I'll find myself standing before the world's best athletes, exhorting them to be godly role models.

Sometimes in those huge arenas or standing in front of all those great men, I reflect on those 5:00 A.M. work details in the early 1980s. Back then nobody stood over my bed yelling, "Let's go, buddy! Move out! Go tackle that roast beef! C'mon, you can do it!" No one sought my autograph for the way I bagged french fries. Yet in those quiet moments, with no fanfare, God formed the character traits of humility and servanthood that I needed to be of any value to Him. That is why the words from Proverbs 18:12 remain burned in my consciousness: "Humility goes before honor."

Diligence

The second crucial attribute for a servant of Christ is diligence. Through constant effort and refusing to quit when the job gets tough, diligence becomes a by-product of the servant's nature. Webster's dictionary defines it as "to choose, to love earnestly." Earnest love for Jesus will cause us to choose to apply God's Word to every area of our lives.

Diligence helps us apply God's patterns and principles without unnecessary delays or negligence. In other words, we put forth constant care and effort to carry out the Lord's instructions. Diligence also serves as a catalyst for maturity and promotes an even temperament. Let's face it: When it comes to "blowing our tops," men are the all-time champs. Many Scriptures address the value of diligence, such as:

- James 1:22: "But prove yourselves doers of the word, and not merely hearers who delude themselves."

- Proverbs 22:29: "Do you see a man skilled in his work? He will stand before kings; He will not stand before obscure men."

- Second Timothy 2:15: "Be diligent to present yourself approved to God as a workman who does not need to be ashamed, handling accurately the word of truth."

- Proverbs 4:23: "Watch over your heart with all diligence, for from it flow the springs of life."

Just as heat causes a cake to rise and solidify as it bakes, in the same way diligence causes our character, disposition, and emotions to rise and firm up. God has provided the ingredients we need to lead a life of victory, but it is up to us to use what He has made available. A lack of diligence will make you a "half-baked" Christian.

A servant must use diligence in every area of life, whether in personal habits, at home with his wife and children, at his place of employment, or in his community. Diligence will inspire you to take charge and bring these areas under control instead of letting them control you. "The hand of the diligent will rule, but the slack hand will be put to forced labor" (Prov. 12:24).

Diligence is vital to producing Christian servants of high character who are willing to lead. Leaders will ultimately be judged not by the commands they issue, but by the content of their character and how well they serve their fellow human beings. And, before anyone is qualified to lead, he must have been tested as a follower, the type who governs himself wisely in shouldering the burden of a goal, cause, or standard of commitment.

Godly leaders must be diligent men of action. They will not be counted among the doubting, whining complainers who cry about their rights and how they are helpless victims. Such moaners know little or nothing of patriotism, civic responsibility, or brotherly service. Wise Christians avoid selfish men of ill-disposition, such as the lazy sailor described by legendary British writer Joseph Conrad (1857–1924):

> They all knew him! He was the man that cannot steer, that cannot splice, that dodges the work on dark nights; that, aloft, holds on frantically with both arms and legs, and swears at the wind, the sleet, the darkness; the man who curses the sea while others work. The man who is the last out and the first in when all hands are called. The man who can't do most things and won't do the rest. The pet of philanthropists and self-seeking landlubbers. The sympathetic and deserving creature that knows

all about his rights, but knows nothing of courage, of endurance, and of the unexpressed faith, of the unspoken loyalty that knits together a ship's company.[2]

A man with a loving, servant-like attitude and diligence becomes a self-governing Christian warrior. Wise self-government is one of the marks of a mature, well-nurtured disciple of Christ—doing what is right even when no one else is around to watch. He is skilled in the art of godly character, knowledge of the Word, and brotherly kindness. He knows the truth of 1 Timothy 3:5: "But if a man does not know how to manage his own household, how will he take care of the church of God?"

Diligence is missing in much of the church today. Its obvious sign is the loss of will for self-government. Too many want someone else to watch over them, pray eloquent prayers on their behalf, and explain the Word to them so they don't have to bother to study it. They explain such shabby, status-quo Christianity with the excuse, "I'm just as good as the next guy. Matter of fact, I'm in the upper 50 percent of good people around here."

We see the same phenomenon physically that we do spiritually. Personal fitness trainers abound in America's health clubs because so many people want someone else to hold them accountable—make them do what they should have done in the first place. When handled properly, accountability is biblical and an awesome concept. But it doesn't mean anything without self-initiative and the will to live as an overcomer.

Likewise, in spiritual matters I hear people constantly whine, "There's no one to help me." That raises the question, *Where did the Lord go?* I hear whiners complain that if they just had weekly marital counseling or a weekly Christian therapy program, then all would be fine. Maybe everything would be fine on the surface. But I have witnessed too many sessions turn into reliance on the counselor with no tangible growth in the counselees. Instead of being changed by the power of God, they get patched up with Band-Aids. Quick fixes never get to the root of the problem, so it keeps resurfacing in a cycle of failures and successes.

Accountability groups and godly counsel are good, but you must guard against the trap of depending on people. I believe a considerable amount of counseling wouldn't be necessary if Christians first went to

God diligently in prayer and sought answers in His Word. (However, if you have taken these steps and remain stuck in a dilemma, then seek counsel from your pastor or other spiritual leader and accept their insights as God's gift.)

God wants His kids to grow up, assume responsibility for their actions, and be dependable servants. To experience personal reformation, men must voluntarily conform to scriptural principles and stop looking for a quick fix or a "patch 'em up" preacher who will somehow tide them over. Trust in the goodness of the almighty God who loves you and wants to strengthen you and enable you to answer His call on your life.

We must be diligent in seeking the Bible's counsel too. Verses like, "Let us therefore draw near with confidence [also translated "boldness"] to the throne of grace, that we may receive mercy and may find grace to help in time of need" (Heb. 4:16). First John 2:27 adds, "And as for you, the anointing which you received from Him abides in you, and you have no need for anyone to teach you; but as His anointing teaches you about all things . . . you abide in Him."

The point of the latter is not a warning against spiritual counselors or church authorities. It is talking about not being deceived. You escape deception and error through the safeguard of the Holy Spirit's anointing. But you must spend time with Him. This is your duty under His lordship and your personal responsibility under self-government.

The fruits of national restoration will be evident when men take charge of their personal lives, families, and civic duties. If you want to make a difference with your influence, then you must first rule yourself. Many try leading our government or culture when their own lives are in ruins. Is it any wonder our nation seems adrift in despair, confusion, immorality, and financial crises?

A healthy nation begins with healthy, God-fearing individuals who can govern themselves. The more a man of God can internalize self-government, the less he will need external rule, whether that be from his wife, children, church, or civil government. And the happier he will be. "If therefore the Son shall make you free, you shall be free indeed" (John 8:36).

Purity

I define purity as someone who is clean in motives and actions. Purity gives you an innocence and allows you to walk in freedom without being nagged by guilt or condemnation. The pure heart contains affections fully surrendered to the lordship of Christ. A man of purity doesn't roam around church, home, and community in a constant search for self-fulfillment. He is thankful for Christ's redemption and, with great joy, is willing to do anything for the Lord.

Purity can come only from a genuine experience of repentance before God. "For behold what earnestness this very thing, this godly sorrow, has produced in you: what vindication of yourselves, what indignation, what fear, what longing, what zeal, what avenging of wrong! In everything you demonstrated yourselves to be innocent in the matter" (2 Cor. 7:11).

God wants to guard the purity of our relationship with His Son. When He holds our affections, His abundant life can flow through ours. But our hearts must not be divided. Impure hearts hold on to pleasurable, sinful habits, make limited commitments, and try to quench spiritual thirst with a hidden lust for things like material wealth, romance, sports, or entertainment.

God has always extended His mercy, grace, and love to imperfect men. And the desire to serve Him will enable you to overcome your weaknesses. When Jesus looked at His disciples and saw the promise that lay beneath these insecure, bumbling men, He thought, "I can use them. Despite their weaknesses, they have hearts for God." You can see the same principle at work when the Lord counseled the Old Testament prophet Samuel. God told Samuel His choice for king was not David's handsome brothers but the insignificant shepherd: "God sees not as man sees, for man looks at the outward appearance, but the LORD looks at the heart" (1 Sam. 16:7).

Who is God looking for in our generation? Do you have the qualifications to fellowship with Him? Psalm 24:3–4 spells them out: "Who may ascend unto the hill of the LORD? And who may stand in His holy place? He who has clean hands and a pure heart, who has not lifted up his soul to falsehood, and has not sworn deceitfully."

If your heart is set on serving Jesus, then your affections will focus on Him instead of your fleshly desires. One way to know if your heart is right is to consider your relationships at home. A husband who constantly demands his own way reaps a house filled with strife. His wife won't meet his expectations and his children drive him up the wall because they don't do things *exactly* the way he wants. Did you ever hear a man fume, "Things aren't going the way I planned around here"? That's the problem. He planned them, not God.

Is your treasure found in Him? If not, you will live with the results of selfish, demanding choices. You will feel unfulfilled and unhappy with yourself and others around you. Depression will be the norm. You will constantly experience overwhelming responsibilities, blame others for your troubles, resent your wife and children, and wonder why life seems so empty. Does this sound like you? Then return to your first love—Jesus.

As men we must war against impure motives. We must guard our hearts from hidden little secrets and dabbling with deception; professing Christian men alone could put a huge dent in the pornography industry by simply avoiding its use. Left unchecked, a man's will and his heart will prove to be his ruin, leading him down bitter roads of compromise. "The heart is more deceitful than all else and is desperately sick; who can understand it?" (Jer. 17:9). The nature of the human heart is to justify impurity, turn self-deceptions into reasonable actions, and lower standards and convictions.

Man either builds the foundations of purity on the inside or pastes it on the outside through personality and charm.

Purity: you either put it in or you put it on. Jesus wants our character to be drawn out of the well of purity residing in our hearts. He warns against men who are merely "whitewashed tombs which on the outside appear beautiful, but inside they are full of dead men's bones and all uncleaness" (Matt. 23:27–28). Man, with his Adamic nature always tries to cover up (Gen. 3:6–8), but God uncovers to clean us up. In other words, man whitewashes but God washes white. Men may cover up, but God cleanses up! Instead of just vain attempts of manufacturing a righteous image (outward appearance), Jesus cleans up our hearts to walk in the newness of life. To walk in purity, we must accept personal responsibility for our sins and rely on God's grace to cause us to be clean.

Conclusion

When we are equipped with humility, diligence, and purity, we are in proper position and always ready to serve God. No request is too small or obligation too difficult because our lives are at Christ's disposal. Whether we live or die we do all for His glory. We must heed the words of our Lord when He said, "Be dressed in readiness, and keep your lamps alight. And be like men who are waiting for their master when he returns from the wedding feast, so that they may immediately open the door to him when he comes and knocks. Blessed are those slaves whom the master shall find on the alert when he comes; truly I say to you, that he will gird himself to serve, and have them recline at the table, and will come up and wait on them" (Luke 12:35–37).

It doesn't take much in today's world to become famous. Fame can come through great exploits, though that doesn't bring us status in God's eyes. Greatness is found in the hands of those who diligently serve. The godly servant has a burning passion to lay down his life and pay any price for the cause of Christ. Oh, that God would give us a heart for discipleship and Christian service the way Michelangelo had a heart for painting. Michelangelo once said, "If people knew how hard I worked to get my mastery, it wouldn't seem so wonderful after all." In other words, great men of God do not just happen but are developed through rigorous labors and selfless service. The Christian servant is the true man of greatness!

Basic Training

- *Humility precedes honor.* (See Prov. 16:18–19; 1 Pet. 5:5–7; James 4:6, 10).

- *Diligence and self-government are the cornerstones of character.* They also represent the foundation of our faith and the substance of great dreams (2 Pet. 1:5–10; Prov. 12:24).

- *Purity converts to power* (Prov. 28:1). The righteous are said to be as bold as lions. Prayer from a pure heart and clean conscience avails much (James 5:16; Prov. 22:11). Purity brings you favor among men.

- You are only qualified to lead to the degree you are willing to serve.

Gut Check

1. Have you taken responsibility at home for the condition of your spiritual life, the management of menial tasks, the nurturing of your wife, and the discipleship of your children? If not, how can you improve? Write down several steps you will take.

2. If you are single, focus on your spiritual life, management of finances, and stewardship of your health and social life. How are you doing in these areas? List several ways that you can improve.

3. Do you know a Christian man you consider to be humble? Can you see strengths in his life you would like to have? Have you considered asking him about the source of his strength?

4. How do you look at your current occupation? Would you like to do something more rewarding? What things are you learning that will be useful in the future? Are you preparing for greater tasks?

5. Are you diligent in carrying out tasks at work and home? Or do you take shortcuts and use the least amount of effort to get by?

6. Is your thought life pure? Do you struggle with lust, bitterness, hatred, anger, and resentment? Do you have an accountability group where you can talk about personal problems and have other brothers pray for you?

6

I'LL BE BACK!

*If the devil sees me coming, he better get out of my way, because I'm on
a mission for Jesus and I don't have any time to waste.*
—A. C. Green, Phoenix Suns Forward

D id you ever dream of standing up for God in a gorilla suit? Neither did I until I went on a mission trip to Australia. I was part
of a group of campus evangelists led by Greg Ball, cofounder of Champions for Christ. We traveled to the University of Sydney to help establish an organization that would have an ongoing gospel witness on that
major college campus.

As part of our series of meetings, Greg organized a seminar titled
"Evolution vs. Creation." Despite the intellectual approach we
thought would appeal to students, few showed up for the first meeting. Putting my marketing degree to good use, I pondered the situation and told Greg to rent a gorilla suit. Then I printed up a
message on an old gray T-shirt and slipped it on. It read, "Is this your
daddy?"

On our next trip to campus I sat on the hood of a car while another man yelled through a microphone, "Ape man, ape man, fact or fiction? Are you just another rung on the evolutionary ladder? Was Cheetah your great-great-grandfather? From goo to you, by way of the zoo." As you can imagine, all this "monkeying around" attracted a lot of attention. The real impact of our effort, however, came in an unexpected way.

When we reached the student center, several hundred student supporters of socialism had gathered and demanded a hearing, trying to gain permission to start a radio station.

As they praised the glories of this godless system, it grieved my spirit. That set off an inner tug-of-war. It felt like the devil was whispering in one ear, "Don't say anything. You're in a gorilla suit. You'll look like an idiot." But the Holy Spirit urged, "You are to be obedient. I'll take the foolish and confound the wisdom of men. Go and be blessed." Jumping down from the car, I yanked off my mask and climbed on top of a bridge overlooking the rally.

"Hey, don't you know this form of government is all washed up?" I shouted through my megaphone. "Any country that has practiced socialism for more than ten years is falling apart at the seams." That drew a barrage of profane insults and cries of "Shut up, you Yankee pig!" But I refused to back down, telling them their actions were typical of socialists. "When someone disagrees with you, you try to silence them," I said. "You want to be heard but don't want to hear anyone else. If you have any sense of fairness, you'll give me five minutes on the microphone. Then I'll be quiet."

Was I ever surprised when they accepted my offer! Though I looked like a hair ball with a human head, the students listened intently as I talked about God's plan for their lives. I told them they would never find their destiny pursuing the most anti-Christian system of government the world has ever pursued. As I spoke, one of the city's major TV stations showed up. How ironic for the rally organizers to see the coverage they hoped for taken up by a Christian proclaiming the gospel. After seeing us on the evening news, the next day one of the rally attendants asked how many people we had on our team. When I told him twenty, he shook his head and said, "We thought you had hundreds."

That marked the turning point in our month-long outreach. God does not need the multitudes to accomplish His purposes, just the committed. When we left we had established a new ministry, which eventually led to several students going on to pursue full-time ministerial callings. The key to carrying out God's plan isn't becoming Superman. It's simply doing the best you can with what you have and trusting God for the results.

Coming Again

"Trust me. I'll be back."

Who said that? Douglas MacArthur? Arnold Schwarzeneggar? Would you believe Jesus? OK, so He didn't quite say it that way, but it is the essence of what He wanted to convey to us. The Ultimate Action Hero had just told of the glorious victory yet to come—the battle when He demolishes the true terminator, Satan, as described in the Book of Revelation.

"'Yes, I am coming quickly'" (Rev. 22:20) was Christ's final promise. He exhorted us that He was coming back; therefore, we are to work while we can to see that His gospel spreads among the nations of the world. As the Lord said, "'We must work the works of Him who sent Me, as long as it is day; night is coming, when no man can work'" (John 9:4).

Even Christ had an appointed number of days on this earth to accomplish the heavenly Father's work and purpose. In like manner, we have a set number of days on earth. Daytime is the proper time for our work, which is to fulfill our God-given destiny and take care of our Father's business.

There will be time to rest when our day is done. At night fall, laborers show the work they have finished and receive their due wages. Because Jesus said, "I'll be back," each of His children should feel a sense of urgency about his or her mission on earth. We should not want to waste one precious moment of our labor to fulfill the Great Commission by spreading the gospel.

Making Disciples

As important as it is to evangelize—tell others about Christ so that they may be converted to Christianity—our job as soldiers of the cross

73

goes much further. We are to ensure that the sacred writings of God's Word are taught to individuals and nations, causing them to rise up, glorify God, and obey His laws.

Bible commentator Matthew Henry, an inspiration to many of America's founding fathers, said this about the Great Commission (Matt. 28:18–20): "What is the principal intention of this commission, to disciple all nations? Admit them, disciples; do your utmost to make the nations Christian nations. . . . The work which the apostles had to do was to set up the Christian religion in all places, and it was honourable work; the achievements of the mighty heroes of the world were nothing to it. They conquered the nations for themselves, and made them miserable; the apostles conquered them for Christ and made them happy."[1]

The foundation of the United States and the influence of Western culture came primarily from men and women who wanted to fulfill this Great Commission, such as Governor William Bradford, leader of the Pilgrims at the Plymouth colony. He once said, "Last and not least, they cherished a great hope and inward call of laying good foundations . . . for the propagation and the advance of the gospel of the Kingdom of Christ in the remote parts of the world, even though they should be but *'stepping stones'* to others in the performance of so great a work."[2]

Even as Governor Bradford embraced the Great Commission, it is urgent that believers in Christ adopt a biblical worldview, one that sees all human labors and efforts as service to God and opportunities to spread the gospel truths. That means a pastor preaching the gospel, a plumber changing a pipe, a salesman marketing his product, and a laborer hoisting fifty-five-gallon drums onto a truck are all serving God. Each person plays a part in furthering God's plan for humanity. Granted, when you're fixing a leaky faucet, calming a crowd of squealing children, or getting an inky face from changing oil, you may not feel too spiritual. But the underlying motive of our labors, creativity, and talents should be to serve Christ and further His kingdom through our witness.

Though as an evangelist I feel a strong devotion to preach the Word, everyone in the church helps spread the gospel. With the tithes and offerings given out of your salary or business profits, you further

God's kingdom. With your good words and deeds you are His witness—a living, breathing representation of Christ on earth. This is what it means to proclaim Jesus, to be a cultural influence for the cause of Christ.

Your authority as a believer extends to every area of your existence. Don't fall for the world's deceptive argument that some areas of society should be strictly secular. Life doesn't have "neutral zones." To assert philosophies or create institutions that are devoid of God's sovereignty makes you hostile toward Him.

Our public schools are a prime example. They claim to remain neutral in matters of religion, values, ethics, and education, but what they have really done is exchange Judeo-Christian morals for the religion of humanism. The Holy Trinity of Father, Son, and Holy Spirit has been replaced by the humanist gods of me, myself, and I. Even the U.S. Supreme Court has long recognized humanism as a religion. In the 1961 *Torasco v. Watkins* ruling, Justice Hugo Black noted, "Among religions in this country which do not teach what would generally be considered a belief in the existence of God are Buddhism, Taoism, Ethical Culture, Secular Humanism, and others."[3] Did you catch that? Humanism. A religion of man finding total fulfillment in self. The humanist says man is the highest order and authority in the universe.

But this arrogant philosophy is contradicted by Psalm 24:1, which says, "The earth is the LORD'S, and all it contains, the world, and those who dwell in it." Did you catch those last five words: "those who dwell in it"? All men and women are God's creation. God is supremely in authority over the universal creation. Humankind is His property and He has a right to His property, right down to the most hard-hearted, arrogant atheist. No matter who you are or what you do, your first job is to act as a divinely commissioned "repo-man," to repossess lost souls.

God's command to preach the gospel and make disciples gives us the right to aggressively pursue people, convince them to turn to Christ, and help them grow in God's family. We have a right and mandate from God to step into the political world, the school systems, the cultural arenas and endeavor to take back that which the devil has stolen and polluted! As Paul exhorts, "Therefore, we are ambassadors for

Christ, as though God were entreating through us; we beg you on behalf of Christ, be reconciled to God" (2 Cor. 5:20).

One mistake Christians often make is looking on Jesus' disciples as extraordinary men. This collection of fishermen and tax collectors was anything but extraordinary. After Peter and John's prayer healed a lame man, Acts 4:13 notes they were "uneducated and untrained." So what is your excuse for not standing up? As A. C. Green says, "This country needs a group of men to lead it out of the wilderness of immorality. But we'll only have such an assembly when men take a stand individually."[4] Remember God's mandate to men in chapter 1? The primary command of Jesus was, "Occupy until I return."

A Cause Worth Fighting For

I love to see God's mandate at work in A. C.'s life. Commenting on his motivation for playing in the worldly arena of the NBA, he once told me, "I view my athletic talents as a musician in our praise group at church would, as a form of worship to God." He told me that he dedicated every minute on the court to the Lord, as his sacrifice of worship for Christ's glory. Not surprisingly, the next night he scored his career high game.

Years ago A. C. set an example that men everywhere still need to follow when he spoke out against pornography in college. When he saw obscene materials sold openly in the campus bookstore, he rounded up a few friends to confront the manager and administration. Despite their stonewalling, A. C. kept speaking out against it, which led to widespread ridicule in the news media and hecklers waving nude pictures at him during games. But A. C. held his ground until this garbage was placed in covered boxes so children wouldn't see it when they walked into the bookstore.

A. C. activated a fundamental principle of boldness: your conscience is one of your most prized possessions, and when your conscience is violated you have a right and a duty to defend it. In this case following his conscience meant speaking out against pornography. On other occasions it may mean taking a stand against the use of foul

76

language by your peers, corrupt practices by a business associate, or the ungodly actions of a political leader. Be a man and take a stand!

Many Christians sneer at the idea of ruling the world. They argue that we aren't of this world and our home is heaven. However, Psalm 115:16 says, "The heavens are the heavens of the LORD; but the earth He has given to the sons of men." After all, someone is going to rule this nation. If not the Christian, then who? The humanists, agnostics, ungodly, perverted, and atheists. We can lose our stewardship over the earth because of fear, apathy, turning our back on responsibilities, or poor theology, but not if we use our faith and jump into the battle for our culture. God will back us up every inch of the way!

After all, Jesus said in Matthew 16:19, "I will give you the keys of the kingdom of heaven; and whatever you shall bind on earth shall have been bound in heaven, and whatever you shall loose on earth shall have been loosed in heaven." He also said, "All authority has been given to Me in heaven and on earth" (Matt. 28:18).

In essence, we have been given divine authority and power to act. When God commands us to make disciples of all nations, He has given us the power to do so. In effect, Jesus is saying, "Come on, church. Go for it. I've dismantled Satan's power. I hold the keys to death, hell, and the grave. Go in the power of My victory, My name, and My authority. Preach My gospel and compel nations to obey Me."

Think of what any believer, or church, could do if they would only believe God's Word. Standing on Christ's authority gives us the keys to cutting off the flow of drugs into this country, shutting down the abortion mills, ridding our streets of crime, and halting child abuse and racism. We hold the keys to economic freedom, educational advancement, and reclaiming moral leadership of the world. Individually, you can't do it all, but at least you can try. Impact your corner of the world for God. Remember the baseball adage, "Nobody ever stole second by keeping a foot on first."

Too many Christians have become apathetic fatalists. They excuse their lack of action by shrugging that the Bible prophesies everything will go from bad to worse until Jesus returns to rescue us. That is not necessarily the case. People have been wrong in the past about the date of Christ's return, so what makes anyone think he can pinpoint the time now? As a buddy of mine once asked, "Why polish brass on a sinking ship?" Well, God's ship isn't sinking! He has given His people authority and He expects us to establish the patterns and principles of His righteousness throughout the world.

When Jesus told us to occupy until He returns, He meant to infiltrate areas that have not been conquered, subdue them for His purposes, and bring them under His lordship. This includes such areas of society as the media, politics, music, and entertainment, which have become moral cesspools. But just because something is bankrupt doesn't mean Christians should turn their backs on it. We are to replace wickedness, filth, and corruption with truth, righteousness, and beauty.

Growing His Government

Isaiah prophesied of the coming of Christ, "There will be no end to the increase of His government" (Isa. 9:7). This passage means that from the time of Jesus' birth, the seed of God's government—His culture and ways—will grow. No power will be able to extinguish that flame and those who try will crumble, as we saw by the fall of the Soviet Union.

The last part of Isaiah 9:7 says, "The zeal of the LORD of hosts will accomplish this." Instead of approaching an assault on evil with God's radiance and confidence, we find an apathetic, sluggish church often retreating in cowardice. We should be living as champions for Christ riding on the cutting edge of faith and standing up for righteousness.

Taking dominion for Jesus in our hostile world today reminds me of watching a Western where the hero gets caught in the crossfire of the bad guys. Instead of sitting idly by and waiting for a bullet to strike, he pursues the outlaw captain with guns blazing, looking for miraculous victory instead of meekly accepting defeat. We need to pursue victory in Christ in this way, daring to be counted among those who overcome (Rev. 3:5). It is better to dare great exploits for God than to shrink back and never try.

The Lord intended for humans to rule over the earth. That is clearly spelled out in Genesis 1:27–28: "And God created man in His own

78

image, in the image of God He created him; male and female He created them. And God blessed them; and God said to them, 'Be fruitful and multiply, and fill the earth, and subdue it; and rule over the fish of the sea and over the birds of the sky, and over every living thing that moves on the earth.'"

God wanted humans to be fruitful and multiply. Since Adam was created in His image, he also inherited God's nature (patterns) and character (principles). God created humans because of His desire for a family who would love Him and walk in His ways. Adam served as His representative to manage the land's resources and guard it from corruption. His three-fold duty on the earth was to (1) fill it—confirm and consecrate it, (2) subdue it—bring it under submission to God's Word, and (3) to rule it—oversee and direct it.

As Christian men we have the same responsibility to exercise God's nature in our homes, society, and culture. At home we are to serve as kings and priests, guarding and governing our families by biblical principles. In society and culture we are to direct, protect, and correct as we promote God's authority. Nothing has changed since Adam. Humans still give account for what the world produces and are to guard it from all manner of evil.

In their rush to avoid the past corruption that marked church power over state affairs, many ministers and laymen have fallen prey to an ungodly philosophy, that separation of church and state prohibits Christians from influencing the state or their surrounding culture. This type of thought violates God's command to disciple nations. Or, as one social observer notes, "When Christians cease to influence the order of society, that society is left to flounder, unprotected against the philosophy of the world."[5]

For example, believers turn away from their responsibility to influence the political world and entertainment industry by labeling them "dirty." They also use that as an excuse to avoid doing anything to clean them up. Neither the political process nor the arts are intrinsically filthy. But both become that way through the corrupt ways of wicked, perverted, sinful people. The problem is compounded by Christians' apathy and neglect when we should act as the nation's conscience. Our participation in government, whether as public official, citizen activist, or informed voter, is not an option. God commanded us to go into the earth, not hide from it.

Have you ever thought about how our nation formed the idea of checks and balances in designing the three branches of government? The judicial, legislative, and executive components of our system reflect God's triune nature as Supreme Judge, Law Giver, and King. Likewise with scriptural influence in the founding of America. Modern historical revisionists are doing their best to censor the Bible from making a formative impact on society and culture. But God's Word was our nation's basis for law, the framework of our government, and the measure of our culture: "When the Reformation swept over Europe, it put the Bible in the hands of the people, revolutionized concepts of government and set the stage for the American Republic," says John Whitehead, president of the Rutherford Institute. "With the influence of Samuel Rutherford, John Witherspoon and John Locke, the Bible became the basis of United States government and law."[6]

This biblical emphasis impacted many of our founding fathers and leaders throughout our history, such as Noah Webster (1745–1843), known as "The Schoolmaster of the Nation." Webster's 1828 dictionary contained the greatest number of biblical definitions ever given in a secular culture. Here are his thoughts about Christian influence on our land: "The moral principles and precepts contained in Scriptures ought to form the basis of all our civil constitutions and laws. All the miseries and evils which men suffer, from vice, crime, ambition, injustice, oppression, slavery, and war, proceed from their despising or neglecting the precepts contained in the Bible."[7]

Imperfect Yet Useful

The point is not that our ancestors were perfect. If they were, we wouldn't have the blot of slavery staining our history. But even in imperfection, our forefathers operated on biblical patterns and principles. They saw themselves as trailblazers for the advancement of the gospel, holding up the torch of reformation, freedom, and moral purity. Yet in the twentieth century we have fumbled the light. Just think of what the influence of godly people would mean at these critical points in modern history:

- In 1925 the infamous "Scopes Monkey Trial" pitted the teaching of evolution against creation. The church was caught flat-footed and ill-prepared as Clarence Darrow argued it was "bigotry for public schools to teach only one theory of origins."[8] The impact of that trial can't be underestimated. Today the theory of evolution is taught as fact and any presentation of God as the Creator of life is banned from most public classrooms. Imagine how an educated, forceful Christian voice more than seventy years ago would have affected the nation today.

- In June of 1962 the nation bowed to the vehement objections of a few God-haters as the Supreme Court declared prayer in public schools unconstitutional. This in a land that claims to cherish the First Amendment, which was passed to *guarantee* the free exercise of religion! Still, the vast majority suffered defeat silently. Today we have more freedom in the classrooms of the former Soviet Union to talk about Jesus in their classrooms than we do in our own homeland.

- January of 1973 saw the creation of legalized abortion on demand. In another march backward, the Supreme Court declared (better to say invented) that since a woman had a right to privacy, the state could not interfere if she wanted to end a pregnancy. The sanctity of life, fashioned in God's image, now falls to the whims of men and women who have decided their judgment is superior to the Lord's.

- Over the past forty years, under the guise of "free speech" and "freedom of the press," peddlers of smut, obscenity, and pornography have assaulted the nation's conscience. By failing to stand against this flood of indecency, we now must fight an entrenched, multibillion-dollar pornography industry. So it is with the rapid spread of casinos and other forms of gambling, forces that swindle billions from people with their seductive get-rich-quick lures.

The evolutionists, atheists, abortionists, pornographers, and organized crime bosses may appear like overwhelming giants. However, don't look on yourself as insignificant when you are clothed with God's power. God wants His offspring to stand for His ways regardless of opposition. When He asks us to fight, the battle is not ours but His. He will deliver and give us dominion over the land.

I saw this truth at a recent Christian men's event sponsored by Ed Cole. One of the pastors who spoke was Robert Owens of Reno, Nevada. He shared how Dr. Cole had radically changed his ministry with this principle: as a young man one is concerned only with responsibility for self, but as he matures he becomes responsible for others. He recalled the challenge Ed had given him several years before: "Robert, when are you going to stop pastoring your church and start pastoring your city?"

Pastor Owens recognized the significance of that statement and assumed responsibility for more than the relatively few members of his congregation. He looked out on a city that suffered from legalized gambling and prostitution and vowed to make an impact. His rapidly growing church has since planted several other congregations around the area and he hosts a television show challenging the area's ungodly, sinful practices.

Pastor Alden Manamtam is another who boldly took action recently in Honolulu, Hawaii, to combat another unhealthy influence. As he strolled through a shopping mall with his wife and daughter, he saw an advertisement in a store window that featured several men's naked backsides. He fumed, "Honey, something ought to be done about this." That's pornographic and has no place in a family mall." Alden assumed responsibility for what was transpiring: "This is my mall, it's in my community, and it has to be stopped."

He immediately went to the manager's office to complain. Dressed nicely, as if he were ready to spend plenty of money, he told the manager, "I'm here representing the families of this community and want you to know an advertisement of that nature will not be tolerated." Initially, the manager tried to pacify him with empty rhetoric, though he finally conceded to placing a label over the men's backsides.

That wasn't good enough. Pastor Al exhorted his church members to barrage the office with complaints. The next week, the objectionable material vanished from the mall and every store in that chain on the island! Sometimes all it takes is for Christians to lay their hands on a wicked establishment and pray in faith that God would vindicate. "Dry up their finances" and "Remove this wicked place" are simple yet effective measures in silencing evil. Pornographic bookstores have closed in various cities after believers walked around them as they prayed for God to act. These kinds of stories never make headlines, but the objective is to chase away the sin, not claim personal glory.

As you read about others who have stood up, the most important decision facing you is whether you will choose to be a man of blessing and action to our nation. I know you can! Continue to the next chapter to see how in order to influence society, you must stand on solid ground at home. The old adage is this: "If it isn't working at home, don't try to export it!"

Basic Training

- *Everything on the earth is the Lord's.* He has created all the people who live here and He has the right to reclaim His property.

- *Every domain is to come under the authority of Jesus Christ.* This means we must export the gospel principles to every nation, institution, agency, and area of life. This includes such fields as education, entertainment, science, economics, and government.

- *Offer your talents to God.* Regardless of occupational roles and other duties, we should view them as reasonable forms of service and worship.

- *Pastors: Stop pastoring a church and start pastoring your city.*

Gut Check

1. What is the primary intention of Matthew 28:18–20?

2. Read Psalm 24:1. What does it mean to hold a biblical worldview?

3. Whether a minister, plumber, businessman, teacher, or other worker, what is your first duty to God? (See 2 Cor. 5:17–20 and 2 Tim. 4:1–5.)

4. What influential areas has God given you to "occupy" until He returns?

5. Study Isaiah 9:7; Romans 8:37; and Genesis 1:27–28. Do you believe you can impact our society and culture, or do you see yourself as polishing brass on a sinking ship?

6. When we find ourselves in the middle of spiritual conflict, what must we remember? (See 1 Sam. 17:47; Ps. 18:30–39; and Ps. 140:7).

7

IS THERE A MAN
IN THE HOUSE?

The family has always been the cornerstone of American society. Our families nurture, preserve, and pass on to each succeeding generation the values we share and cherish, values that are the foundation for our freedoms. . . . The strength of our families is vital to the strength of our nation.

—*Ronald Wilson Reagan, 40th President of the United States of America*

The atmosphere in our home settled over us like soggy storm clouds dripping with frustration. Our stack of unpaid bills were like a pack of vultures ready to devour every scrap of our resources. The phrase "one day at a time" took on a brand new interpretation. But my wife and I didn't know how many more of these kind of days we could endure.

Have you ever felt the weight of continuing financial pressure? Nothing can create a more dreaded chill in a home. To add a little spice to the mood, Dana was pregnant with our second child and experiencing morning sickness. Feeling as though the world might cave in momentarily, I blurted angrily, "Honey, if it's called *morning sickness*, why does it seem to last *all* day?"

Evidence of our sagging spirits mounted next to the bills. The dishes in the sink resembled the Leaning Tower of Pisa. Clothes spilled out of baskets onto the laundry room floor. Even the dog needed a bath. As if we didn't have enough problems, I felt flu symptoms attacking my body. I felt like throwing up my hands and screaming, "I quit!"

After momentarily swimming in a sea of self-pity, a phrase I often preach shot through my mind: "Champions don't give up. They get up!" So did the words of Ed Cole: "You don't drown by falling into the water. You drown by staying there."[1] In the midst of my anxiety, depression, and weariness, the Ultimate Warrior—Jesus—wanted me to rise up, stand on His Word, and fight for change. As men, God calls us to be the priests of our homes. He wants us to forget circumstances and let the authority of His Word dictate the spiritual climate.

The Bible enables men to become spiritual thermostats. Ever consider the difference between a thermometer and a thermostat? A thermometer simply reads the climate, rising and falling like ocean waves. But after a thermostat examines conditions, in the hands of its master it changes the temperature. One measures reality while the other determines it.

I was tired of acting like a spiritual thermometer. Things were getting too hot. It was time for the thermostat to kick in. Searching for relief, Dana took off for the afternoon to enjoy her favorite sport: shopping! Not wanting these problems to ruin my time with our oldest son, I asked Stephen if he wanted to bloody the devil's nose. Effervescent, five-year-old eyes shining, he squealed, "Yeah!"

I explained that we had some problems, but as we pray and quote God's Word, the Bible becomes a sword of power in our hands. As I mimicked the moves of a master swordsman, I said, "It slices, dices, and minces the enemy into harmless shreds." The devil's attempt to oppress our home couldn't stand up against a relentless prayer of faith, I said. Pointing to my son's Bible on the counter, I commanded, "Sergeant Stephen, pick up your sword!"

Then we marched from room to room. We strode upstairs to our bedrooms and the study, hiked down to the garage, and circled around to the patio. All the while we held our Bibles in the air like swords. In the name of Jesus, we declared, "Sickness, financial distress, disputes, depression, lust, and anger will not reign in our home." I also read verses like:

- John 14:12: "Truly, truly, I say to you, he who believes in Me, the works that I do shall he do also; and greater works than these shall he do; because I go to the Father."

- John 15:7: "If you abide in Me, and My words abide in you, ask whatever you wish, and it shall be done for you."

- Proverbs 13:21: "Adversity pursues sinners, but the righteous will be rewarded with prosperity."

- John 16:24: "Until now you have asked for nothing in My name; ask, and you will receive, that your joy may made be full."

After each Scripture we shouted, "Take that, Satan!" We jabbed and swished our Bibles as if they were clashing metal swords. Afterward, beads of sweat ran down our faces. Stopping to catch our breath, we knelt and thanked God for the results, quoting Psalm 95:1–2: "Let us shout joyfully to the rock of our salvation. Let us come before His presence with thanksgiving. Let us shout joyfully to Him with psalms."

Next I asked Stephen to listen carefully and see if the Lord said anything. After a few moments of reflection, he jumped up and grinned, "Dad, I saw Jesus. He was karate chopping the devil and kicked him in the chest until he disappeared." It reminded me of Psalm 8:2, "From the mouths of infants and nursing babes Thou hast established strength, because of Thine adversaries, to make the enemy and the revengeful cease." What a wonderful memory.

Sound too "far out"? I believe this activity lines up with the seven realities of God at work, as outlined in Henry Blackaby and Claude King's masterful Bible study, *Experiencing God*. Step four says that, among other things, the Lord speaks by the Holy Spirit through the Bible and prayer. God had just spoken to us. That became evident by the change in our home's spiritual climate. Ever since, we have periodically "cleaned house" this way, and it has changed our lives. In addition, that day I learned a valuable lesson, summed up by Bill Marriott Sr.: "Men grow making decisions and assuming responsibility for them."[2]

Strong Husbands

God wants the heads of His families to be strong, decisive, and consistent in their roles as priests, prophets, and kings. The only way men can do that is with a solid foundation. Ed Cole sums up that truth this way: "Every man is limited by three things. The knowledge in his mind. The strength of his character. The principles upon which he is building his life."[3]

The guiding principles that keep us on the right path are what enable husbands to meet the challenge of serving as God's delegated authorities. Husbands are to bond the home into a cohesive unit that witnesses of God's glory. This is the same mandate the Lord gave to Adam. We are to serve as caretakers, providers, protectors, and disciplinarians.

After more than ten years of marriage, I have come to realize that family life has taught me rich, continuing lessons about loyalty, patience, virtue, self-sacrifice, understanding, perseverance, and other positive character traits. When Dana and I married after college, I never dreamed I was enrolling in lifetime graduate school. Amusing, but true!

Today a combination of biblical illiteracy and selfish lifestyles have caused men to ignore their responsibilities as head of the family. Weak husbands lead to wives feeling neglected, children embracing harmful rebellion, and homes crumbling in chaos. And this disaster is not confined to the United States. A 1995 *New York Times* story described women in Russia becoming accustomed to raising children without any help from the fathers. Sociologists cited Soviet oppression, regimentation, and lack of freedom for men's alcoholism and apathy toward work and family. One female television reporter commented, "People tell me I'm so strong, such a heroine. I'm not strong. It's our men who are weak. They have no sense of responsibility."[4]

Ironically, while the world points to the symptoms of family problems, it fails to see the root cause. God designed the family to reflect His kingdom. If Satan can undermine men and usurp their leadership role, he can discredit God and invalidate His structure. The reason the enemy fights the family—the crown jewel of creation—so viciously is that the Lord uses this institution of family to demonstrate His kingdom authority, structure, order, and principles.

Healthy families do more than raise children. They export gospel truths to a dying world. Look at the call on Abraham as the head of his family. He changed the world by bringing it the news of God's eternal covenant. This is outlined in Genesis 12:3, "And I will bless those who bless you, and the one who curses you I will curse. And in you all the families of the earth shall be blessed." God's central plan to redeem all of mankind would operate through the family. That is powerful!

As you consider how the father of Israel affected history, don't forget your own role. You will leave behind a positive legacy or a negative impression. Whether future generations count your family a blessing or a curse depends on what you do now. An example comes from the following story contrasting the godless Max Jukes with the great Colonial-era theologian Jonathan Edwards (1703–58):

> Max Jukes lived in New York. He did not believe in Christ or in Christian training. He refused to take his children to church, even when they asked to go. He has had 1,026 descendants; 300 were sent to prison for an average term of thirteen years; 190 were public prostitutes; 680 were admitted alcoholics. His family, thus far, has cost the state in excess of $420,000. They made no contribution to society.
>
> Jonathan Edwards lived in the same state, at the same time as Jukes. He loved the Lord and saw that his children were in church every Sunday, as he served the Lord to the best of his ability. He has had 929 descendants, and of these 430 were ministers; 86 became university professors; 13 became university presidents; 73 authored good books; 7 were elected to the United States Congress. One was vice-president of his nation. His family never cost the state one cent but has contributed immeasurably to the life of plenty in this land today.[5]

This century has seen a tremendous assault on biblical, family values. Today's humanistic, self-centered generation heaps scorn on the traditional family as an outdated institution that deprives individuals of personal freedom. It is true that imparting family values requires a sacrifice of time and effort. But how can we ignore the societal benefits that result, such as long-lasting marriages, good homes, stable neighborhoods, and peaceful cities? Couples who endure life's challenges together and lovingly nurture children can positively influence them so they have a much better chance of becoming happy, confident, productive citizens.

Since family is strategically important in furthering God's government, we can expect Satan to dishonor it. So, it is not surprising that evil, anti-God attitudes mocking family, marital fidelity, and purity are a staple of popular entertainment. Commenting on how history shows those who capture the fantasies of the masses rule the world, Larry Poland, the leader of a ministry to Hollywood, laments the influence of modern media luminaries:

> Rock stars and pop musicians stir the passions of America's youth to sex, drugs, rebellion and rock and roll. The soaps capture an opulence of lifestyle and an abandonment of sexual mores that seduces a generation of daytime TV addicts. Hugh Hefner and Bob Guccione sell slick, lying images of unbridled and guiltless sexuality and nudity. Oliver Stone moves us to passionate distrust of government and rewrites history with his distorted images of everything from the Vietnam War to the assassination of JFK. Arnold Schwarzenegger and Bruce Willis glorify the annihilation of our enemies by sheer firepower. Beavis and Butthead and Bart Simpson define enlightened attitudes for children. Corporate advertisers move us to covetousness on a grand scale with irresistible fantasies of sleek, new machines, grand mansions, sartorial splendor, rich and extravagant delicacies, trim bodies, and even odorless underarms.[6]

But the media is not alone in attacking the family. The ungodly doctrines of feminism have ingrained negative images of the traditional family in the public's consciousness. Writers like Kate Millett, author of *Sexual Politics*, argue the family must go because it oppresses and enslaves women. How sad for feminists to equate a hallowed institution with slavery because they have no grasp of the godly definition of authority and servanthood.

Others are fighting viciously to redefine the family, particularly gay rights activists and other special interest groups. They argue same-sex marriages, multiple partners (such as two men and one woman), and other combinations are normal, acceptable behavior. Sometimes it seems that society views the conventional practice of man and wife together as abnormal. Well, as one who appreciates how morality shaped our nation, I don't believe supporters of Judeo-Christian ethics have the problem!

House Trap

The assault on family values has created a house-trap philosophy that turns the wedding ring into a shackle, reduces marriage to a battlefield for control, views children as inconveniences, and devalues women as mere sex objects. How ironic that scoffers routinely portray Christians as chauvinists who oppress women. The truth is only when a man is born again does he discard the uncaring use of women and esteems them as equal partners and co-heirs in Christ.

We can see the results of the attack on marriage and glorification of self through the namby-pamby spineless men it has produced.

Do you know a young, married man whose marriage stands on shaky ground because he refuses to grow up, won't assume responsibility, and complains their crying baby robs him of sleep? And, instead of dealing with these pressures, he dumps them on Mom while he hangs out with the boys? I do. This tragic story can be repeated in any town, city, and state.

Such whiners may be males by birth but they aren't men by God's standards. These men view their mates as second-class citizens who perform the so-called menial task of child rearing while they bring home the bread. When a man fails to honor his wife and accept his duties as a husband and father, he may think he is the breadwinner, but he is really the heel. Heels also refuse to help with domestic chores and treat family time like an infringement on their pleasure.

I have watched such men in action. Like the father who, when his children asked if he would take them to a funny kids' movie, sneered, "Don't talk to me. That's your mother's job." On another occasion, he was running baseball drills with his son and some friends. When they got sidetracked by the sight of some bugs, he barked, "All right, if you aren't going to work at this and would rather play, I'm out of here."

The only thing that man was "out of" was out of line. He was too much of a macho man to go to a kiddie show or play with bugs. But true strength allows a man to be gentle. Real masculinity will inspire a

91

man to enjoy his children and step into their world instead of forcing them to walk lock-step with his self-image.

Scenes like this are why I am convinced society needs to think less about self-fulfillment and more about self-denial. Only in sacrificing our self-interests and wants will we find the enjoyment we crave. Fulfillment does not come by focusing on self but through turning our eyes on others, starting in the family. By ranking others' needs above our own and nurturing their destinies, we will meet a Christlike standard. In John 10:11, Jesus called Himself the good shepherd: "I am the good shepherd; the good shepherd lays down His life for the sheep." As husbands and fathers, we need to follow this example and shepherd our flock.

Men, if you have been worried more about yourself than about those God has entrusted to your care, it is time to change. Gain a hold on your home. Earn the respect of your wife, children, and community by embracing godly masculine authority. Don't be a dominating glory hog. Exemplify a biblical servant filled with wisdom, maturity, discipline, and grace. Be the kind of man who leads his family and covers them with prayer, guidance, and the security of his attentions and affections.

For the ultimate warrior, the acceptance of responsibility is the benchmark of maturity. Family order comes when a man submits himself to Christ. Your wife and children will gladly follow a loving, godly man. But no one wants to submit to someone they don't respect. That is why it is crucial for a man to set the example of a godly, disciplined life. It takes a real man to declare, as Joshua did, "But as for me and my house, we will serve the LORD" (Josh. 24:15).

It also takes a real man to nurture his family and create an environment where each member reaches his or her unique destiny. Sacrifice yourself for them. Sure, you could be doing something other than watching *Barney* for the hundredth time or playing GI Joe (or worse yet, Barbie!). But the most precious investment you can give your children is time with Dad. Some of my sons' greatest growth has come from talks and lessons that emerge as we play together. Selfish, insensitive fathers will miss these opportunities to shape young minds. Also they'll miss out on some incredibly fun times.

How do you view time with your family? Is it a burden or a delightful investment in the next generation? Giving your family time demonstrates caring and respect for them. You may not realize how precious these moments are, even if you don't look at them that way. Children build their foundation for the future on today's memories and the examples they see.

Ultimate Warriors

The Ultimate Warrior. Sounds so macho, bold, and glamorous. But in reality, God's effective warrior must be centered in principles and girded by character. Before our call to be warriors, we were called to a family of believers who had accepted Jesus Christ as Savior. Natural family has been a part of most of our lives from birth. We understood family roles before we even knew our own name.

Family is the single most important factor and safeguard in the longevity of successful warriors. Those who try to face challenges on their own become spiritual orphans and casualties. They will burn out before realizing their destiny or weaken their convictions until the enemy demolishes them. Family is vital to a warrior for stability, security, nurturing his strength, and providing times of refreshing. In turn, a godly warrior strives to be a man of character for the sake of his family. He dreams God's dreams, dares to accomplish His purposes, and passes an inheritance to the next generation—a spiritual and cultural inheritance that is considerably more valuable than money.

A warrior finds strength in church family too. Our church (MorningStar International) rallies together under its mission statement: "To train Christians to be leaders who will impact the world with the gospel of Jesus Christ." Any good Christian leader will share similar stories of the strength gained from his or her local church. A common vision, goal, and purpose gives each believer power to accomplish God's will in our spheres of influence. God attracts like-minded men and women, with similar spiritual DNA, to produce a segment of His family known as the church. Warriors are called to be part of this kind of local fellowship.

Today's attack against family stems from a rebellious spirit that refuses to acknowledge God. The ultimate warrior on earth, however, recognizes the only way he can fulfill his role of priest in the home is by submitting to the lordship of Christ. Trying to establish strategies, implement discipline, and set morals and values without His guidance is useless. Psalm 127:1 says, "Unless the Lord builds a house, the builders' work is useless. Unless the Lord protects a city, sentries do no good" (TLB). Thus, a man has three primary duties at home:

1. *A man must live in submission to Jesus, who is the family's Chief Architect, Master Builder, and Premier Protector.* The biblical pattern comes from James 4:7: "Submit therefore to God. Resist the devil and he will flee from you." Ed Cole puts it this way: "Habits, good or bad, are developed or broken by submission or resistance. What is submitted to grows stronger, while what is resisted from grows weaker."[7]

A man under Christ's lordship is qualified to exercise authority and discipline. He knows he is accountable to God for his actions, and if he acts unfairly the Lord will correct him. The Bible says in 1 Peter 3:7 that if a man doesn't treat his wife with understanding and honor, his prayers will be hindered. When he operates with respect for God and his helpmate, he is fit to direct his home.

2. *A man must pray for his wife and children.* Ed Cole has long taught how prayer produces intimacy: "You become intimate with the One to whom you pray, the one for whom you pray, and the one with whom you pray."[8] Physical intimacy that lacks the spiritual oneness of prayer is like a man who prepares to run a marathon by cutting off his right leg. Whether marriage, family, or occupation, you will never outgrow the boundaries of your prayer life.

Why is this intimacy so important? Because the greatest gift you can give your son or daughter is to love their mother. You need to tell her consistently, in their presence, that she is God's gift to you. A man without tangible, visible love for his wife will raise dysfunctional children who lack stability, security, and guidance. Your children may not always listen to you but you can be assured they will imitate your example. The kind of legacy you create helps determine whether marriage will be restored to a place of national prominence.

3. *A man must use the Word of God as his home's source of truth.* Millions of families are disintegrating because they don't know the Bible. As priest you must lead family devotionals and encourage personal quiet times

with God. You will never know where you are going unless you get your guidance from the Son of God as revealed in His Word.

Don't be like the men who are too busy to listen. After hearing me preach about Israel wandering in the wilderness for forty years, one woman quipped, "I know why it took forty years for them to enter the Promised Land. Men were leading and they wouldn't stop to ask for directions." The importance of the Bible cannot be overstated. It will instruct you about marriage, your mate, children, occupation, and personal relationships. You cannot hear the instruction if you don't listen.

If you don't spend time with God you will fall victim to self-delusions. I remember a period in our marriage when I had quit listening to Dana. When our pastor asked me after our weekly softball game how our marriage was going, I would smile, "Oh, fine, just fine. Couldn't be better." Later in the week when he posed the same question to my wife, she gave him a much different perspective. This discrepancy came from my failure to give her enough of my time. When communication with your wife and children stops, I can guarantee that abnormality will soon set in. My neglect caused me to see a mirage of a marriage.

But what is the difference between my blindness to reality and men who fantasize about their spiritual health? Ask a man if he is the home's spiritual leader. Then take his wife aside, ask her, and compare answers. Most men would be shocked at their mate's response. It is only through daily Scripture reading and study that we will be able to accurately assess our relationship with God.

As James 1:23–25 says, "For if any one is a hearer of the word and not a doer, he is like a man who looks at his natural face in a mirror; for once he has looked at himself and gone away, he has immediately forgotten what kind of person he was. But one who looks intently at the perfect law, the law of liberty, and abides by it, not having become a forgetful hearer but an effectual doer, this man shall be blessed in what he does."

The supreme test of God's ultimate warrior is whether he meets God in His Word each day. Jesus said, "If anyone loves Me, he will keep My word" (John 14:23). By faith, if you will plant the seeds of God's Word in your heart, His Word will do a work in you and your family. The Word is the catalyst for change and the power behind growth: "For this reason we also constantly thank God that when you received from us the word of God's message, you accepted it not as the word of men, but for what it really is, the word of God, which also performs its work in you who believe" (1 Thess. 2:13). We will focus more heavily on this in chapter 12.

Home Sweet Home

When irresponsibility gives way to godly men walking in their priesthood, it rekindles flames of love, replaces rejection with acceptance, and knits estranged children back into the family fabric. Through examples of lordship, intimate prayer, and Bible study, we will see the fulfillment of these prophetic words, "And he will restore the hearts of the fathers to their children" (Mal. 4:6). Such a man instills masculinity in his sons, confirms femininity in his daughters, provides security to his wife, and directs his family in the Lord's ways.

When enough homes are transformed through God's love, we will see a revolution in our society and culture. Just as God ordained a natural family for you to be birthed into, so it is with God planting you in a church. From this base you can change the world. Your roles as father, husband, and brother in Christ are not in vain. Let your family be a shining light in the midst of a cruel, dark world.

Remember, if you fail to become the head of your household under the Lord's direction, someone else will take your place. If you don't set domestic policies, then your wife will. Or your children. If not them, then the government. Someone will step in to fill the vacuum.

We desperately need Christian men who govern their homes wisely to get involved in city councils, boards of education, county commissions, state legislatures, and Congress. If we continue to cling to isolation, tolerance, and apathy, we will fail in the task the Lord has set before us. The times demand action and sacrifice, just as they did in the days of Nehemiah. God placed Nehemiah, an Old Testament prophet, in a position to promote the revival and restoration of Israel. Jerusalem had been devastated by war. The protective wall around the city had been destroyed and its people were in despair.

The Book of Nehemiah describes a situation that vividly parallels the 1990s. Our spiritual walls have been torn down by corrupt, evil men and their ungodly practices. As Nehemiah's generation rebuilt Jerusalem's walls, their enemies slandered, threatened, mocked, and accused them. But Israel overcame antagonism and persecution to accomplish God's plan, all because of the strength of their families. Nehemiah 4:11–14 spells it out:

> And our enemies said, "They will not know or see until we come among them, kill them, and put a stop to the work." And it came about when the Jews who lived near them came and told us ten times, "They will come up against us from every place where you may turn," then I stationed men in the lowest parts of the space behind the wall, the exposed places, and I stationed the people in families with their swords, spears, and bows. When I saw their fear, I rose and spoke to the nobles, the officials, and the rest of the people: "Do not be afraid of them; remember the Lord who is great and awesome, and fight for your brothers, your sons, your daughters, your wives and your houses."

What a model! We need men with their families stationed by our broken-down spiritual walls, fighting to establish God's reign. We need husbands, fathers, and leaders with eternal vigilance who will stand for God's ways. Men who receive their commission as heads of families and yield to God's call will receive rich rewards.

The greatest inheritance you can leave for posterity are children who walk in God's ways with His sense of destiny filling their lives. A real man's lasting value will come from the time and energy he sows into his family. Your time is short. Spend it wisely.

Basic Training

- *You don't drown by falling into the water. You drown by staying there.*

- *God wants every man to guide, guard, and govern.* He is the priest, prophet, and king of his home.

- *Healthy families raise more than children.* They serve as models to the world and export gospel truths to the lost (Gen. 12:3).

- *God's plan for family is to bless future generations.* Following godly standards today will affect ancestors who haven't even been born.

- *Gentleness is a sure sign of masculinity.* A truly strong man is not afraid to be a sensitive husband and a nurturing father.
- *Contentment comes from self-denial, not self-fulfillment.*
- *Acceptance of responsibility is the benchmark of Christian maturity.*
- *Family is vital for the longevity of a warrior.* This includes church family as well as immediate and extended family.
- *Children are our greatest investment and future resources.*

Gut Check

1. What are your responsibilities as the head of your home? See Ephesians 5:25–29; 1 Timothy 3:4 and 5:8.

2. Describe how you care for your wife and discipline your children. Have you provided for your family emotionally and spiritually, as well as financially? If you have been selfish in stewarding your family, stop now and ask God for forgiveness.

3. What impact did the story of Max Jukes and Jonathan Edwards make on you? What kind of legacy do you hope to leave? List some ways that your family is impacting the world for God.

4. Homosexual-rights activists are lobbying to obtain the legal right to marry and be considered "family," which will give them an even stronger voice in public school curriculum. What are some of the traditional family values that are under attack in your community? Are you speaking up in favor of traditional families?

5. What is the benchmark of a man's maturity?

6. How can you strengthen your responsibilities as a husband or father? List three practical steps you plan to take.

8

LEARNING
TO LOVE A FIGHT

Americans love to fight. All real Americans love the sting of battle. . . . You give me ten good men unafraid to die and I can destroy an enemy division of ten thousand. That is, if the ten men will stay awake.

—General George Patton

Victory! USC had just won another afternoon clash on the gridiron, but more exciting things lay in store that evening. A revival was stirring on the football team and several players wanted to visit Westwood to do some open-air preaching. Home of the UCLA Bruins, Westwood also hosts some of the nation's largest movie premieres. On a typical Saturday night, crowds flocking to the west Los Angeles restaurants, clubs, and theaters lend it the air of a party center.

We arrived on a main street corner around 8:30 P.M. Surprised by the unusually calm atmosphere, I glanced around and said, "OK, I'll kick it off. Let's go." One of the players, Marlon Washington, laughed, "Kick what off? There are three trees, a fire hydrant, and a dog!" I didn't care. As team chaplain, the Lord had given me a message that needed to be delivered.

Now, I can get pretty loud when I preach in public. Former Harlem Globetrotter star Meadowlark Lemon calls me "The Human Lung." Bracing myself, I inhaled deeply and belted out a hurricane-force cry, "Woooooeeee! It's Saturday night and I'm ready to party! Who wants to raise some hell tonight? C'mon, let's raise some hell!"

Then I raced around the four corners of the intersection like a wild man, chanting, "It's party time!" Slowly, bodies gathered on one corner. From a dozen the numbers steadily grew to several dozen; after awhile, it appeared a few hundred eyewitnesses had appeared. Westwood cruisers are used to street performers and sideshows. They wondered what was happening. With one more urgent blast I said, "Who wants to raise some hell tonight?" A great cheer went up.

About that time the corner was filled and I clarified my calling. "OK, you want to raise hell. But I'm here to r-a-z-e hell. Raze means cutting down, tearing up, and overthrowing. I want to raze hell and establish God's kingdom on earth." Watching mouths drop open and shoulders sag, I expected the majority to leave. But the crowd mushroomed until we had to split into several witnessing teams.

Not that we didn't face opposition. At one point hostility erupted and two guys crept up behind me with beer bottles. But two of our men (Steve Webster, our star tailback, and Lou Brock Jr., one of our starting defensive backs) raised their fists and challenged, "Whatcha gonna do?" and the would-be attackers slipped off into the night. When Keith Davis, later a teammate on the Power Team, approached another mocker, the man fled, exclaiming, "Dude, I ain't messin' with any man whose neck is bigger than my thigh!"

Several persons gave their hearts to Christ and dozens more opened their hearts to the good news for the first time. I am so proud of the men who stood up with me that night. They are true heros of the faith. On the way home our men were more excited about whipping the devil that night than a football opponent that afternoon. Just then I sensed God's still, small voice encouraging, "You were born for battle, son. You were born to raze hell."

These men had the warrior's spirit! God has placed it in each man's heart. God's man is not someone who fights with fists, guns, knives, or nun-chuks. He is trained in using the spiritual weapons of prayer, faith, and proclaiming God's Word. This takes commitment, dedication, and perseverance. Jeremiah 48:10 warns, "Cursed be the one who does the LORD's work with deceit, and cursed be the one who restrains his sword from blood." As we have mentioned, every man has a mission and should be doing the Lord's work. In doing so, you may need to pull your sword of the Spirit, God's Word, and draw blood (Eph. 6:17 and Heb. 4:12). We become negligent when we hold back telling the gospel truth to someone because we are afraid of an unpleasant conflict.

Confrontation

Men, you have been created for such a time as this. Today's crumbling family structure, rampant immorality, drug and alcohol abuse, widespread gambling, and violent crime have created an unstable society wracked by fear. It is up to men to confront this evil and chase it from our midst. Yet, most men have a desperate fear of confrontation and seek to avoid it. Nobody likes confrontation. It is messy, inconvenient, uncomfortable, and sometimes hostile. Yet it is vital. Confrontation is a natural element in the progression of our character, the security of our nation, and the advancement of humankind throughout the course of history. We must not fear when God wants us to draw our swords. This is a key element in the discipleship mentoring process.

When I say you must confront others, *I do not mean* to be critical, bullying, controlling, complaining, gossipy, or divisive. Confrontation must be loving and seek to restore others to a relationship with God and reconciliation with others. The model is found in Galatians 6:1–2: "If a man is caught in any trespass, you who are spiritual, restore such a one in a spirit of gentleness; looking to yourselves, lest you too be tempted. Bear one another's burdens, and thus fulfill the law of Christ."

Communicating the gospel accurately during confrontation takes three essentials: words, gestures, and spirit.

All three must be in harmony. For example, it is not enough to deliver a doctrinal statement of beliefs solely in word. If the gestures of our lifestyle and the spirit of our character don't agree with our words then others will correctly label us hypocrites. Likewise, if we cling to legalistic, ritualistic obedience to God's law without remembering His love and grace, we become self-righteous. The true warrior for Christ matches his words with actions and attitudes.

Here is another example. I do not believe any Christians should blindly bow to the moral excuses of abortionists, the perversion of homosexuals, or the legislative remedies of the immoral and godless. But we must not retaliate with firebombs, venomous speech, or self-righteous pride. We may have a zealous spirit, but our gestures are misguided, disqualifying our witness. Jesus said the meek shall inherit the earth. *Meek* doesn't mean *weak*. Meek refers to a humble man walking in the spirit of Jesus' love. Like Jesus, he doesn't tolerate sin, yet he loves sinners and intercedes for them. Proper confrontation can only come from those whose words are true, their gestures are from love, and their spirits are found pure. This type of man will walk in the power of Christ Jesus.

One of my favorite World War II heroes is General George Patton, who embodied the warrior spirit. He was not afraid of confrontation. His fellow soldiers told of him putting on his "war face" before going into battle against the Nazis. I remember that phrase whenever I face a difficult task, such as the time John Jacobs challenged me to try a new feat before a huge crowd in Tulsa, Oklahoma.

It called for me to run full speed at a stack of five two-by-fours, held by two 300-pound bruisers. I was to snap the twelve-foot-long boards in two across my chest. I put on my war face and braced myself. Keith Davis patted me on the back and said, "Tom, there are 15,000 people here tonight. You're going to hear one of two sounds when you hit those boards. You're either going to hear everyone in this arena cheering wildly or you're going to hear them say 'Oooooooooohhhh . . .'" So much for moral support!

That night all I could think of was those boards. Finally my turn came. John screamed, "No fear! You can't have any fear. Don't you hesitate! Run through them, Cannonball!" In unison with the two men holding the boards, I rocked back and forth on my feet as John sounded the count, "One . . . two . . . three!"

Boom! I shot across the stage. *Wham!* I hit those two-by-fours harder than anything I ever hit, including the massive offensive tackles in college. Instead of breaking, the wood imitated a rubber band and flung me backward like a human sling shot. I landed on my shoulder and backside. As Keith had forecast, a huge "oooooooooohhhh" sounded from the crowd. John stood with his mouth hanging open and the microphone dangling at his side.

I staggered to my feet, my left side entirely numb. Suddenly the Lord gave me a Scripture. Grabbing the mike, I quoted Micah 7:8, "Do not rejoice over me, O my enemy. Though I fall I will rise." "How many of you know that even when you are living for God or have a dream in your heart that sometimes you may get knocked down?" I asked the audience. "But you just have to get up! You may get knocked down but you're not knocked out. God says to get up and hit it again."

Seized by inspiration, I declared, "Let's do it one more time, John." Then I blinked my eyes and thought, *You idiot, you almost got killed the first time.* But Keith came over to urge, "Go for it. You've got'em, Tom. You cracked every board on the first hit." His words filled me with vigor. On my next run, I smashed through and splinters flew. The crowd exploded in cheers as I leaped onto my teammate Siolo's shoulder, triumphantly waving my fist.

You don't have to cut down a stack of lumber with the flex of your chest to know similar pain. Just when you are striving to fulfill your destiny or see a dream come true, you get attacked by sickness, job setbacks, marital strife, rebellious children, or accidents. It feels like someone drop-kicked you in the gut. Discouragement, depression, and fear of failure settle over you like a wet blanket. However, just like my first attempt in the arena, this is not the time to grow faint-hearted.

My first run through the two-by-fours was a painful and embarrassing disaster. Yet because of the cracked wood, I had only to make another effort. Instead of sulking in defeat, I enjoyed victory. So it is with life. If you've been knocked down, get up and hit it again. You may have already cracked the surface and God is ready to give you the breakthrough if you won't quit and will confront the problem one more time. Whether it is your job, marriage, family, destiny, dreams, or influencing our society, God calls you to attack with faith and stand firm in hope.

Patton's Principles

A warlike disposition causes a man to make commitments and sacrifices as he lives for a cause bigger than himself. A man with a warrior spirit will find the courage to go beyond his limited abilities and strive to do better. This is the type of spirit that made General Patton's troops some of the most feared during World War II. Toward the war's end, many German troops threw down their weapons to surrender at the sight of Patton's tank brigades. His typical speech went like this: "We are lucky people. We are in war! We have a chance to fight and die for something. A lot of people never get that chance! Think of all those poor people you know that have lived and died for nothing. Total lives spent doing nothing but eating, sleeping, and going to work until the gold watch is received. We are ——— lucky to be fighting a war that will change history. If we live, we can put our grandchildren on our knees and tell them we did it! If we die, our friends can tell how we died to make life better for them. If you are going to die, you might as well die a hero. If you kill enough people before you die, they might name a street after you."[1]

Whether in times of conflict or peace, you need a warrior spirit to carry you through life. If you don't think this kind of strong stance sounds like God, look at His nature. Zephaniah 3:17 describes Him as "a victorious warrior" in our midst. Revelation 19:11 calls Christ "Faithful and True; and in righteousness He judges and wages war." First John 3:8 says, "The Son of God appeared for this purpose, that He might destroy the works of the devil." Romans 16:20 tells us "the God of peace will soon crush Satan under your feet."

The warrior spirit is an oft-neglected image of God's nature. Yes, God is love, but at times the best expression of His love comes clothed in a zealous warrior spirit. God's love for His people, patterns, and principles led the prophet Isaiah to declare, "The LORD will go forth like a warrior, He will arouse His zeal like a man of war. He will utter a shout, yes, He will raise a war cry. He will prevail against His enemies" (Isa. 42:13).

In Isaiah's era, God was looking for a man to stand in the gap, but He found very few. In that corrupt era, materialism reigned, people had no fear of God, innocent people were being killed, and the civilization was in disarray (sound familiar?). Not many things shock an all-knowing, all-seeing, all-powerful Lord. But He was surprised by the situation in Isaiah's day. The prophet describes it in Isaiah 59:15–17:

"Now the LORD saw, and it was displeasing in His sight that there was no justice. And He saw that there was *no man*, and was *astonished* that there was no one to intercede; then His own arm brought salvation to Him; and His righteousness upheld Him. And He put on righteousness like a breastplate, and a helmet of salvation on His head; and He put on garments of vengeance for clothing, and wrapped Himself with zeal as a mantle" (emphasis added).

God is still looking for men to rise up, defend the cross, promote His redemption, demonstrate His power, and establish His purposes. He wants men to be imitators of Christ. The words of 2 Chronicles 16:9 are still true today: "For the eyes of the LORD move to and fro throughout the earth that He may strongly support those whose heart is completely His." Yet, the good news is that God doesn't expect you to rely on your own strength. Look at the arsenal of weapons He has provided, listed in Ephesians 6:14–17:

- truth to wear around your loins
- a breastplate of righteousness
- the preparation of the gospel of peace to wear on your feet
- the shield of faith
- the helmet of salvation
- the sword of the Spirit, which is God's Word

We must put on this armor to wage war with the devil. A football player wouldn't dream of running onto the field without shoulder pads and a helmet. Neither should you face your spiritual enemy without protection. In this fierce battle we are called to overthrow Satan's plans. Ephesians 5:11 commands us to expose "the unfruitful deeds of darkness." *Expose* means to *convince, rebuke,* and *reprove.* We are to confront the world with the truth of the gospel.

One such soldier is Clay Shiver, a '96 graduate of Florida State University (FSU). Before Clay began his senior year, *Playboy* magazine called FSU's athletic department to say they had selected him for their pre-season All-America team. Think of how most college players would crave this worldly prestige, publicity, and great notice with professional football scouts before the following spring's pro football draft.

However, Clay had different ideas. Challenged by team chaplain Clint Purvis to think it over before *Playboy* even called, he prayed and came up with an answer: "No thanks." Explaining his decision, he said, "God just burdened my heart with the fact that I would be double-minded if I called myself a Christian and did it. *It would be like supporting a magazine of that type.* I didn't see any way I could do it."

Shiver may have given up a chance for public acclaim but in doing so he made God's first team. Not only would participation be an endorsement of this pornographic magazine; he didn't want to embarrass his family or give his friends an excuse to buy it. In addition, he realized the responsibility resting on him, quoting Luke 12:48: "And from everyone who has been given much, shall much be required."

These are the leaders society needs, men who refuse to bow down to worldly ways and have the courage to cut against the grain. Strong men draw firm lines and declare, "I don't care what anyone says. I will not compromise my integrity or God's Word by crossing this line."

Full-Contact Christianity

Some of you may be thinking, *Wait a minute. I didn't sign up for any fights. I just wanted a smooth ride to heaven.* Friend, wrestling with the enemy is part of the spiritual arena. Only those who know Jesus Christ as Savior will leave the auditorium victorious. Scared? You would be crazy not to tremble at the thought of facing powerful foes.

Nevertheless, the battle is on. When you read about such calamities as two young men in Chicago killing a five-year-old by dropping him off a building, street gangs across the country spraying gunfire at innocent bystanders, and children in Texas beating a horse to death with sticks, you are seeing the results of a root of spiritual wickedness. That is why you must develop a warrior disposition.

The warrior heart will enable you to stand up against opposition. It reminds me of our old cat, Solomon. A playful bundle of whiskers, he purred softly if you scratched his head and trembled like a bowl of Jello when you stroked him behind the ears. But rub his coat the wrong direction and suddenly this furry feline flicked his claws out like switch-blades.[2]

Remember Solomon when you point out society's perverse ways. Not many will mind if you follow a Christian philosophy in private, especially if you keep it behind the church walls. But speak out publicly and the world's toothless lions roar with disapproval. You have rubbed them the wrong way and they are ready for battle. Still, you have nothing to fear. Matthew 10:28 says, "And do not fear those who kill the body, but are unable to kill the soul; but rather fear Him who is able to destroy both soul and body in hell."

For the battle-tested warrior, fights are not something to fear but to anticipate. They are a chance for God to demonstrate His power. You should gladly receive times of testing and additional responsibilities as a normal part of maturing. In the words of 1 Peter 4:12, "Beloved, do not be surprised at the fiery ordeal among you, which comes upon you for your testing, as though some strange thing were happening to you."

There is an old saying that men are like tea. You have to throw them in hot water before you can see their strength. Spiritual battles test our hope in Christ, build strong faith, and produce useful men for the Master. Unless a man fights, he is easily seduced by comfort and forgets about his duty to serve God. However, the Lord understands this tendency, so He uses enemies, trials, and temptations to strengthen our resolve.

"Teach Them War"

Second Samuel 22:40 shows God's design for us: "For Thou hast girded me with strength for battle; Thou hast subdued under me those who rose up against me." In other words, God declares, "Teach them war!" (Judg. 3:1–4). He wants men to stand up and fight to fulfill their destiny, protect their homes, guide their children, and influence their society. Why should we settle for less when it comes to God's promises? I don't intend to let Satan steal, kill, or destroy the best of me or my family.

Think about it. Why should we let this culture's Goliaths go unchallenged? Evil only triumphs when uncommitted, passive, immature babes in Christ are afraid to lay it on the line. You must risk everything you have, from finances and reputation to honor, status, and credibility, for the sake of the gospel. If you don't think God believes in taking strong stands and fighting enemies, then consider these words from Psalm 144:1: "Blessed be the LORD, my rock, who trains my hands for war, and my fingers for battle." In war there is no substitute for victory!

Jesus, the Ultimate Warrior, was such a man. I believe we need to hear more about the Jesus described in Revelation: eyes like flames of fire, feet of burnished bronze, a voice like mighty, rushing waters, and a face that shone like the sun. He spoke with such power that John described it as a sharp, two-edged sword coming out of His mouth.

Jesus is the Ultimate Warrior, the Lord who confronts sin, condemns unrighteousness, and delivers justice. At times we, too, must accept the mantle of a warrior. God's church was established to reign in the midst of our enemies, not to passively retreat from them. Churches must influence their communities for good, not blindly seek their approval or yearn for political acceptance. God's people are to serve as moral agents and cultural engineers.

Lakita Garth and Adam Peacocke (Dennis's son) were like two spies who were sent to scout out the promised land and come back with a report. "We can take these guys" was their motto as they headed to Paramount Studios. The panel discussion was Hollywood vs. Washington, D.C., and how the two could better their relations.

Lakita, part of the Hollywood community, said, "The entire entertainment field is running scared that the new wave of conservatism is going to result in the tight censorship of Hollywood." Each of the major networks had a representative in attendance, along with producers, actors, and political figures from around the country.

When concerns by those holding Judeo-Christian or traditional family values came up, some of these producers became quite condescending in their tone. "I don't want anyone to tell me what I can and cannot produce." "If you don't like it, turn the ———— thing off" was another angry comment. Someone else chimed in, "Haven't you ever heard of economics? You know, supply and demand. We're just giving people what they want."

Lakita said that that was all she could stand, and before she knew it, she was on her feet confronting one of these big-name producers and informing him that the top ten money producers from the 1980s were rated G or PG except for one. She said you should have seen their faces when there was no screen to hide behind. They were unable to stand up to the truth. Hollywood wasn't giving us what we wanted but was constantly ramrodding their evil inventions and philosophies down the public's throat.

"You're not giving us what we want. We want good family values, characters with substance, and wholesome lifestyles. Since 90 percent of the top grossing movies are G or PG, why are you spending 60 to 70 percent of the time producing R rated films? That's not good economics!"

"But, but, we can't find any scripts," was his only flimsy defense.

Lakita shot back, "Then I'll see you right after the panel discussion to submit you a few." Lakita obtained an appointment and discussed the possibilities for an action film script with biblical principles throughout. What an open door! The people in attendance for the discussion flocked around Lakita and Adam afterward to find out more.

"It amazes me how there is such a hunger for truth," she said later. "It's time for someone to stand up. We are waiting for God to move. Well, He's waiting for us. It's ours for the taking."

God has given us a sword to touch society, but too many men leave it lying on the ground to rust, or they put it in a showcase for display. They have filed their swords down until all they have left is a butter knife. Yet Hebrews 4:12 says, "For the word of God is living and active and sharper than any two-edged sword, and piercing as far as the division of soul and spirit, of both joints and marrow, and able to judge the thoughts and intentions of the heart." That is power!

Remember, we shouldn't shy away from confronting others with God's Word. Its double edge means it has two sides. One side is love, grace, mercy, and forgiveness. But God also has a wrath more fierce than anything on earth. Only when you grasp what God has saved you *from* can you appreciate how much His love means.

A Man of Arms

As I thought about my experiences on the athletic field and the history of war, I compiled a list of character traits I have noticed in a man of arms. You may have your own, but my image of such a man includes one who can

- handle crises,
- solve problems,
- deal with insecurities,
- meet needs,
- adapt to change,
- persist through hardships,
- maintain poise,
- control his temper,
- rise to a challenge,
- defend his convictions,
- resist evil,
- confront injustice,
- make sacrifices,
- live for a cause greater than himself.

These are worthy qualities for all men, young or old. They appeared in Jesus' life, which is why I refer to Him as the Ultimate Warrior. He came to our world in peace, preached a gospel of love, healed the sick, and cast demons out of people. He could have raised up an army against the Romans, but He became a meek sacrifice for the sins of humankind. Was a warrior spirit at work in Him? Absolutely!

Just look at our Savior in light of His deeds:

- Jesus dealt with crisis and insecurity on the eve of His crucifixion. Agonizing over His fate in the garden of Gethsemane, His sweat became like drops of blood (Luke 22:44). Yet He did not run from the mob when the Romans came to arrest Him. He went to the cross, proving His willingness to live, and die, for a cause greater than Himself.

- When He fed the multitudes (Matt. 14:13–21 and Mark 8:1–10), Jesus adapted to change in feeding people when no source of food was readily available. He also demonstrated great compassion as He met both physical and spiritual needs. He provided the crowds with food to eat, but also nourishment for their souls by giving them answers and solving problems.

- There was no bigger challenge than the one He faced on the cross. Nobody had ever met this test, nor will anyone else meet it in the future. Christ demonstrated incredible courage and bravery, conquering all opposition and persisting through hardship.

- Jesus controlled His temper before Pilate and King Herod (John 18:28–19:11) and maintained His poise, even though He faced charges for crimes He never committed.

- When He delivered the Sermon on the Mount (Matt. 5–7) He spelled out truth and stood on His convictions.

- He resisted evil after the Holy Spirit led Him into the wilderness to be tempted by the devil. Even when weak and tired after forty days of fasting, He faced Satan head on and fought for His destiny (Matt. 4:1–11).

- Jesus confronted injustice on many occasions, such as when He cleaned the temple (John 2:13–17) and during His frequent confrontations with the Pharisees (for example, Matt. 23:1–32). These passages show how a perfect Man, filled with love, can be filled with zeal and righteous anger over sin and hypocrisy.

In every dimension of Jesus' ministry and personal life He manifested warrior-like traits. These are the same ones that can be evident in your life and sphere of influence. As I mentioned in our first book, *Warriors*, David surrounded himself with mighty men "who understood the times" and had "knowledge of what Israel should do" (1 Chron. 12:32). The biblical pattern shows that when righteous men rule, the people rejoice (Prov. 14:34; 28:12; 29:2).

God is looking for men of action. If you are a Christian, the Holy Spirit dwells in you. So does the wisdom of God. Your mind has been renewed and you are in fellowship with the Creator of heaven and earth. This gives you awesome potential to bless others and the capacity to solve problems and crises. If anyone should have the answers and can serve as a role model in this troubled, sin-polluted world it is a man of God!

Instead of wringing your hands over the plagues of drugs, gangs, pollution, disease, economic burdens, educational crises, eroding moral standards, and fading family values, treat them as invitations to witness for God's glory. To paraphrase the words of Mordecai in Esther 4:14, "You have been created for such a time as this."

You were created by an all-knowing God. It is not by accident that He placed you in this generation. He sent you as a conduit for change and a facilitator for righteousness. Daniel said, "The people who know their God will display strength and take action" (Dan. 11:32). Do you want to be that kind of man? Remember what you need to do:

- Don't fear confrontation.

- Assume responsibility for your life. Problems will always exist in your home, marriage, career, and society. They will only be solved by strong men who rely on God's grace to change.

- Dare to lead by being a positive influence in your family, workplace, and social spheres.

- Go on the offensive by knowing God and His Word.

- Be willing to be a trained soldier (1 Pet. 5:6–10).

- Embrace faith and shun fear by remembering 1 John 5:4: "For whatever is born of God overcomes the world; and this is the victory that has overcome the world—our faith."

- Base your convictions on God's Word. Don't be swayed by men's preferences, political correctness, or popular opinion.

- Develop a willingness to serve and lay down your life for the cause of Christ. Get involved in your church, community, and social issues.

Now is the time to win nations for the Lord. These are desperate times, and we must have men who will go the extra mile and take action. Saints of God, it is time for war! Read the following Christian disciple's manifesto (a declaration) out loud, preferably with your men's group:

We, the disciples of Jesus Christ, avow a day of reckoning in our society and culture at large, a calling to account of the worldly forces of darkness and the spiritual forces of wickedness who would act to violate and deny the law of God.

With a clear conscience and in conjunction with fighting the good fight of faith, we boldly accept the Lord's challenge to stand up for Him against evildoers and those who do wickedness. We reply in the words of the prophet Isaiah, "Here I am, Lord. Send me."

As an act of militancy, in a declaration of war with our spiritual enemies, we assault the secular values and worldly institutions of this age. By using the weapons of righteousness and aggressive faith, we will prayerfully await for divine opportunities to take action and achieve great exploits.

In an era of Christian bashing, bigotry, and intolerance towards believers in Christ, we countercharge the humanistic, anti-Christian ideologies of our times. In holding to and protecting our most sacred convictions we oppose all who would subvert the Judeo-Christian ethic and values, and all those brainwashing this generation with a tide of secularism and atheism. We stand against those who would undermine normalcy by substituting perversion and rebellion, and by mocking and misrepresenting the godly.

Finally, to those who gravitate to retreat and compromise in our religious institutes, to the inventors of evil, to the puppets of the devil who call good evil and evil good . . . we, the blood-bought soldiers in the army of God, declare war and do most solemnly promise to *"occupy until He returns!"*

Basic Training

- *Every man has a mission.* No matter how you earn a living, you are called to do God's work. As Dr. Martin Luther King Jr. said, "If a man hasn't discovered something that he will die for, he isn't fit to live."[3]

- *Confrontation can be pleasant.* Correcting others in a spirit of gentleness and love is a chance for both sides to grow. We go on the offensive when we know God's Word.

- *Meekness is not weakness.* It takes a strong man of humility to walk in a spirit of Christian love.

- *When you get knocked down, get back up.*

113

- *Your convictions matter.* Even when you think nobody notices, others are watching you to see how you act in various situations and react to pressure.

- *God is looking for men of action.* Because the Holy Spirit lives in you, you have a renewed mind and the capacity to solve problems and crises.

Gut Check

1. What are some memorable past battles you have won—spiritually, athletically, occupationally—through confrontation or competition? What did it take? Write them down.

2. Who are some of your warrior-like heroes? What admirable, spiritual qualities do they have?

3. Are you afraid of confrontation in your home, workplace, school, or community? What type of disciple should you prove to be? (See Prov. 28:1; 30:30.)

4. A confrontational spirit does not mean overzealous anger, judgmental attitudes, or hostile challenges. What are the attributes of a godly spirit of confrontation? (See Gal. 6:1–2 and Matt. 7:15–21.)

5. Read the story of Phineas in Numbers 25:1–13. Then focus on verse 11. What warrior-like quality did Phineas have that turned back God's wrath?

6. Names some areas where God has called you (put a burning desire in your heart) to go to battle.

7. What should you do when you get knocked down as you pursue your dreams, goals, and destiny? (Read Micah 7:7–8.)

9

A GENERATION
OF GIANT-KILLERS

The Lord gives us friends to push us to our potential—and enemies to push us beyond it.

—Jim Vorsass

To those living in the twentieth-century world, this story is sad, though very common. Highways stand deserted as travelers seek alternative ways of crossing the land; marauding bands of thieves and plunderers instill fear in the hearts of law-abiding citizens. Public safety is but a dim memory. Business and commerce are negatively impacted. Nearby rural fields lay desolate and untilled, since farmers frightened by constant violence no longer work in their fields. Valuable wells sit idle because a trip for water might result in personal attack. Justice has yielded to bribes and oppression. Residents have no peace, day or night. They are so depressed they lack both the means and spirit to fight the criminals.

What metropolis do you think this describes? Washington, D.C.? Los Angeles? Chicago? Atlanta? Maybe a faraway place like Rio de

Janeiro, Brazil; Calcutta, India; or Berlin, Germany? None of the above. This was the state of affairs in Israel thousands of years ago, after the nation fell victim to the cruel invasion of the Philistines: "In the days of Shamgar the son of Anath, in the days of Jael, the highways were deserted, and travelers went by roundabout ways. . . . New gods were chosen; then war was in the gates. Not a shield or a spear was seen among forty thousand in Israel" (Judg. 5:6, 8).

Amid this atmosphere of despair an obscure farmer emerged to challenge the enemy. Shamgar, too, lived in the subhuman surroundings, while indignation and righteous anger brewed in his heart.

I can envision him lurking in the shadows as he traveled, thinking, *This isn't right, crawling on my belly. I've had enough!* Everywhere he could see starving family and friends and once-productive farms deteriorating into wastelands. Deciding he had endured too much, this farmer harnessed his ox and resumed work. *Matthew Henry's Commentary* says he was probably behind the plow when the Philistines invaded the countryside, and God put courage in Shamgar's heart, leading him to oppose them.

Since he had neither sword nor spear, he used his oxgoad. Over eight feet long, it had a small spade on one end and a sharp point on the other. Showing the courage of a lion, Shamgar attacked. What could one man, so vastly outnumbered, hope to accomplish? It didn't matter. He refused to live like a prisoner any longer. Better to die fighting than to live in humiliation and fear.

When combat concluded, Shamgar stood tall and unharmed. Around him lay six hundred dead Philistines. More important, his courageous act signaled deliverance for God's people. Who would have thought this farm boy could prove so valuable to the Lord's work? God. He has the power to raise up millions or rely on one brave soul. A touch of His Spirit can turn plowmen into judges and fishermen into generals of faith.

Shamgar was an average man who simply used the tools he had to tackle an awesome task. Today we must ask God to also transform us into the same kind of warrior. It seems we, too, face an invasion of Philistines in the media, politics, entertainment, the arts, and science.

Despite these bleak conditions, the sounds of revival are stirring. God is placing in men's hearts the will to oppose these dark giants. And

116

our nation is crying out for even more men to wear Shamgar's mantle. We don't need pew sitters from the First Church of the Nonoffensive. God wants giant-killers who aren't afraid to stake their reputations, finances, and their very lives to overthrow evil and raise a standard of righteousness. Charles Swindoll once exhorted, "There is only one you. God wanted you to be you. Don't you dare change just because you're outnumbered."[1] Shamgar remained faithful to what God put in his heart. Will you?

Want a Piece of This?

Legendary football coach Vince Lombardi once said, "The will to win means nothing unless you have the will to prepare."[2]

You must be trained for battle. It isn't enough to just want to kill giants. Unless you are trained and equipped, you will get chewed up and spit out.

God wants His men so rooted and grounded in His ways of thinking that faith, convictions, and understanding of His patterns become reflex movements. You rehearse them over and over again until they become part of you. It is easy to act tough while singing war songs around a campfire, but the true test of toughness comes in the fight when you can feel the sting of battle.

I'm convinced on the day we stand before God He won't ask about our diplomas, badges, or medals. He will ask to see our battle scars. In football, we called them stick marks. When a player made a good hit (a stick) on an opponent, he came away with paint from that man's helmet stuck to his own. Those battle scarred helmets denoted the toughest players. The only one on the team who wanted a clean helmet was the kicker.

Likewise, we are called spiritually to the "good fight" (1 Tim. 6:12), to punish the enemy. Though we must withstand hits, we need the toughness to strike offensive blows. I want to get into the game against the devil and collect some stick marks on my helmet of salvation. You should too. Christians were meant to occupy positions of leadership in society. We must kick the devil out of man's affairs and reinstate God's patterns and principles in the world. I remember one bold evangelist saying, "I want to be on hell's most wanted poster! If the devil doesn't start something with me when I get up in the morning, I'm gonna start something with him. As a pastor that's the type of men I'm looking for. Those who upon arising in the morning cause all of hell to tremble: 'Oh no, he's up again. What is he going to do to us today?'"

In the same light, Colossians 2:15 shows how Jesus celebrated His victory over the forces of darkness: "When He had disarmed the rulers and authorities, He made a public display of them, having triumphed over them through Him." See the pattern? (1) Disarmed. (2) Made a public display. (3) Triumphed. Christ has already won! Yet, many are looking for Jesus to do at His second coming what He has already accomplished. Instead of moaning over the devil's attacks, we should remind Satan he is a defeated foe.

My friend Dennis Peacocke leads a ministry in Santa Rosa, California, called Strategic Christian Services, which is committed to educating and mobilizing Christians for effective community service in order to spread the gospel. He outlines the fighter's perspective in taking on satanic giants this way:

1. *Interpret:* Determine what kind of an attack you are facing and what forces are involved.

2. *Engage:* Determine the technique required to fight. For example, the technique may be prayer, fasting, or coming in a spirit opposite of the one attacking you.

3. *Succeed:* Determine how far you will go to win and what you will do. Advance decisions will help you provide the determination to follow through with swift action.

The battle against the forces of evil is not a show, but a fight to the death. It's not something you do Sunday morning and forget the rest of the week. Peacocke says, "Satan won't waste his time on folks that don't even give him heartburn." Are you doing anything that is worth the devil's opposition? Some Christians think they are fighting spiritual warfare when, in reality, they are simply paying the price for violating scriptural principles. Others are engaged in genuine character-building exercises initiated by the Holy Spirit.

Serious warfare erupts when a person is hurting the enemy's grip on the earth. Christian action makes sparks fly. You will never know that kind of battle without a systematic strategy and consistent commitment. The will to fight giants doesn't come from increasing your I.Q. It comes from having more "*I can*—do all things through Him who strengthens me" (Phil. 4:13, emphasis added). And there are plenty of giants out there. Let's look at a few examples.

Abortion. When Congress voted in 1995 to outlaw partial-birth abortions, feminists and others raised an outcry against this alleged invasion of a woman's right to privacy. But abortion's supporters weren't willing to face the truth. During this procedure a doctor pulls the baby's feet out of the womb and leaves the head in the birth canal:

> The baby is still alive, its toes still wiggling. Its little legs still kicking. Then the doctor slips a sharp instrument—often scissors—to puncture the baby's head. Then the brain is suctioned out. The skull collapses, and the baby—if it hasn't already—finally dies. The corpse is withdrawn from the mother . . . and discarded. . . .
>
> Why do they keep the baby's head inside the mother during such a vicious procedure? Because it makes the procedure technically legal. Since the baby is still alive, if the head emerges, the medical procedure would most likely be regarded as murder under the law. As columnist John Leo says, this is little more than "a legal fig leaf." It's hardly abortion any more. . . . It's infanticide. Legalized baby-killing. Murder for convenience. . . . If we do not put a stop to this butchery, we allow our country to slip even closer to total moral self-destruction.[3]

Disrespect for Family. We see this throughout the entertainment industry and media at large. Just because a practice is widely accepted in our culture doesn't make it right. Measure His Word against the casual acceptance of unmarried couples living together, which is a violation of the commandment, "You shall not commit adultery" (Exod. 20:14). (Adultery is defined as sex outside of marriage.) Hebrews 13:4 reads, "Let marriage be held in honor among all, and let the marriage bed be undefiled; for fornicators and adulterers God will judge." Illegitimacy has skyrocketed to over 30 percent of all births, which threatens the very definition of "traditional family."

God doesn't ask our opinions on morality, nor does majority vote determine right and wrong in His Book. He sets the standard; we either meet it or reap the disastrous consequences. He ordained the traditional family—husband, wife, and children (and sometimes grandparents) living under the same roof—but the modern rush by the liberal elite to discard family as society's centerpiece is ripping the heart out of America.

Disrespect for the traditional biblical family has propelled us down a path of immorality, confusion, and despair. We cannot endure this type of gross perversion for long. The Roman Empire fell because of moral decay; what the Roman enemies could not accomplish through outside force was achieved through internal ethical and moral decay. By ignoring the lessons of history we stand a great risk of following in Rome's footsteps. By speaking out for God's ways and setting a good example, you can counteract these forces. Small, seemingly insignificant decisions by millions of Christians create a major impact.

Situational Ethics. On a shopping trip I overheard a teenage clerk tell her friend that although she was a good Catholic girl, she saw nothing wrong with moving in with her boyfriend. "Yeah, living together used to be wrong, but not any more," her friend agreed. When I checked out I leaned over and whispered, "By the way, it's still wrong." After reminding her what the Bible says, she meekly admitted, "Well, I guess you're right."

This store clerk reminds me of the college professor who once told me, "Everything is relative. There are no absolutes."

"Are you absolutely sure?" I asked.

"Absolutely," he responded, then flinched in red-faced embarrassment at his inherent contradiction.

I continued to goad him, "I say you are 100 percent, absolutely a male."

The professor responded smirkingly, "That's not necessarily so."

"What do you teach?" I demanded.

"What does it matter to you?" he responded, seeming agitated.

"Because I don't want to sign up for a class next year where my professor can't even tell whether he is a male or female." Needless to say the debate was over as he stormed off in disgust. This professor shows how the philosophy of relativism has cast a hypnotic trance over our society, usually in the name of tolerance and diversity. "If it feels good do it." As long as it is good for you and doesn't hurt anybody else it's OK.

Actress Demi Moore reflected this philosophy in the cover story for the June 1996 issue of *George*. Promoting her latest movie, *Striptease*, she defended the lifestyle of exhibitionists by saying, "Obviously what inspired me to play Erin was that you captured a character who was up against the wall, who had a skill she could make money at, and she wasn't compromising her integrity. The strongest feminist statement I can make is: Be supportive of women who make conscious choices for themselves. That's my job as a woman: to support women in their choices, not in my judgment of their choices."[4]

Situational ethics and relativism's bankrupt outlook has influenced every niche of society, from education and the arts to government, to the point that to speak against it brings ridicule, ostracism, and false charges of anti-intellectualism. It is no wonder the world invented the humanistic theory of situational ethics. Its creed has spread through the misnomer of "values clarification," which is nothing more than a blatant attempt to destroy and redefine all sense of values. Men who can't handle the truth about their sinful, lustful cravings will fight to the death to convince others those actions are normal. As 1 Peter 4:4–5 says referring to the godless, "And in all this, they are surprised that you do not run with them into the same excess of dissipation, and they malign you; but they shall give account to Him who is ready to judge the living and the dead."

Situational ethics is a giant that must be rooted out of our society and culture. Relativistic doctrines that downgrade moral absolutes are such a pervasive part of American society that it will take heroic efforts to overcome them.

Homosexuality. This immoral habit is rapidly gaining acceptance in mainstream America. I don't want to encourage anyone to harshly condemn those caught up in this practice. I know of Christians who fight incredible struggles against desires for a person of the same sex. Often, a root of childhood molestation is to blame. (Note: for a thorough exploration of this issue, read *Unwanted Harvest* by Mona Riley and Brad Sargent, Broadman & Holman, 1995.) Nor should we overlook the fact that homosexuality is not any different than any other form of lust. Still, that does not mean we should shrug it off or ignore it.

I have heard homosexuals excuse their behavior by saying some members of the animal kingdom engage in it. Does that mean we should also imitate the animals who eat their young? While we need to help those who want to leave homosexual lifestyles, we must recognize that same-sex relationships degrade the family order that begins with one man and one woman.

Meek acceptance, often because of fear of attacks by militant activists, has contributed to the decline of morality. If you don't speak out against harmful influences in the hope of protecting your corner of the world, what will you do when the spreading tides of indecency wash over you?

A new term has emerged in the nineties called D. D. Down (Defining Deviancy Down); the removal of homosexuality from psychiatry's list of deviant behaviors is a prime example. This trend is reflected in the attitude of the store clerk I mentioned earlier. Deviancy has become so widely accepted in our culture that to cope with the consequences, we redefine normalcy. This leaves us with a floating system of morality that rises and falls on the whims of public opinion. Currently, homosexuals are fighting to obtain minority status for political and legal power along with passing legislation for states to recognize same sex marriages. The destructive force of such entitlements would be immediately felt in our public schools. Same sex marriages would open the doors of adoption much more readily for homosexuals and give them power to be much stronger in their demands to redefine sex education and the traditional family role that would be taught to all children.

Racism. Racism is another giant, still plaguing the United States more than a century after the Civil War. Slavery left a dark stain on American history. Our forefathers penned the then-revolutionary idea that all men were created equal, with certain inalienable rights. But the political compromise that failed to outlaw slavery ultimately led to vicious war. The church played a role too. As Promise Keepers (PK) founder Bill McCartney noted at the 1996 PK Pastors Conference, "If the church had 'come together in harmony before God, racism could never have taken hold.'"[5]

The consequences still divide our nation today. Slavery helped birth the demonic racial hatred that continues. How else can one explain the cowardly burnings of dozens of black churches across the nation in 1995 and '96? The hatemongers' targets included the Knoxville, Tennessee, church where NFL All-Pro Reggie White is an associate pastor. After they destroyed the church, White said the arsonists were still phoning the pastor with death threats. But he declared they wouldn't hurt him.

"No more of our leaders are going to die off because of people who hate," he said. "We aren't going to be the kind of Christians who people walk up to and slap around. We are not going to walk around in fear. Nobody is going to make me and my family afraid. . . . It's time to stop sweeping this stuff under the rug. If we don't do something about these groups, more people are going to die."[6]

This kind of attack is why I am encouraged by groups like Promise Keepers and others who actively promote racial reconciliation. Building bridges of understanding is a Christian's duty. There is no excuse for hating anyone based on their color. First John 4:20 says, "If someone says, 'I love God' and hates his brother, he is a liar; for the one who does not love his brother whom he has seen, cannot love God whom he has not seen." The vision of heaven in Revelation 7:9 adds, "After these things I looked, and behold, a great multitude, which no one could count, *from every nation and all tribes and peoples and tongues,* standing before the throne and before the Lamb, clothed in white robes, and palm branches were in their hands" (italics added). It was Booker T. Washington, in an address in Boston on May 31, 1897, who said, "The black man who cannot let love and sympathy go out to the white man is but half free. The white man who retards his own development by opposing the black man is but half free."

Violent Crime. According to a 1995 Louis Harris poll, violent crime is so prevalent it affects behavior, expectations, and school performance of teenagers nationwide. One in four don't feel safe in their own neighborhood; the ratio jumps to one in two in high-crime areas. One in three worries about being a victim of a drive-by shooting. More than 70 percent in high-crime areas say that gangs play a major role in the daily life of their neighborhood.[7] During a recent school assembly with the

Power Team a teacher was asked what her goals were for the upcoming school year. "Staying alive" was her reply.

A Call to Men

The facts themselves issue a call to Christian men. The nation stands on the precipice of disaster. To use a baseball metaphor, we must step up to bat and swing at evil. Our future depends on it. What can you do? Pray for our nation and ask God where you can be a witness and be of service to your community.

Talk to your pastor too. Discuss avenues he sees for your talents and abilities. Maybe you are a good athlete and young boys need a coach for their games. Perhaps you can put together a newsletter to inform your church about prayer requests and local, state, and national issues. Whatever the church, there is never a shortage of available tasks.

One of the most urgent needs in our nation is for mentors and big brothers to help guide young people. Commenting on the Harris poll that showed widespread fear of crime among teens, John Calhoun, executive director of the National Crime Prevention Council, said, "From a policy perspective these figures say to me that kids really long for and need adult connections. This country has a huge reservoir right under its nose that's ready to help."[8]

The basic formula I learned in marketing applies: *Find a need and fill it.* There are many ways in which wholesome, God-fearing people are needed to stand up:

- participating in marches and rallies like "Washington for Jesus" or the "See You at the Pole" campaign each fall

- carrying signs in pro-life rallies

- passing out tracts and writing informed, well-planned letters to the editor

- writing letters to local newspaper editors, Congress, the president, and local and state representatives on family, moral, and social issues, and voting in elections

- giving to worthy causes that daily face down the giants. (Since you pour your life into earning your wages, your money is precious to

God—not because He needs it but because it represents something of great value to you.)

- educating yourself so that you can handle opposition and be a spiritual workman who speaks the hope of the gospel and dispels the enemy's lies with biblical reasoning and truth

- short term missions (Many churches as well as groups like Ron Luces's "Teen Mania" provide excellent opportunities.)

All Dressed Up and Nowhere to Go

Each generation has its own giants to fight. Years after Shamgar slew hundreds of Philistines, the same outlaws were oppressing Israel (1 Sam. 17:19–21). David's father, Jesse, ordered him to take supplies to his brothers. They were supposedly in a dogfight against the enemy and their number one man, the giant Philistine Goliath.

As David approached the camp he heard the warriors giving the war cry and talking it up. That is, until they saw Goliath. I can imagine David's shame as he came upon the scene and watched his "home boys" chickening out at the sight of the giant. Israel looked like a frightened kid backed into a corner by a schoolyard bully, too afraid to fight. All too often the church has taken in error the same stance primarily through either *retreat* or *accommodation.*

Retreat. By withdrawing from all levels of society and culture, we nullify the Lord's influence. Civil law, the arts, economics, government, and education are spiritual in nature and subject to God's Word. Unless Christians stand in the gap and profess God's ways, evil sweeps in without restraint. Satan and his hellish forces have declared war on the world. Our choice is to fight or get overrun. The church must learn to love the smell of battle. The church, by and large, abandoned areas such as Hollywood and national politics because they were dirty. Is it any wonder we suffer from the corruption and filth? My prayer is that God would send His soldiers into these arenas once again. I recently came back from an appointment with one high ranking congressional staffer who pleaded with me to exhort men of godly character to dare to run for office. He said, "Tell churches that there are some men of God daring to fight for godly reform. But at times we feel like the little boy with his finger stuck in the dyke. We can't do it alone much longer." He closed out our conversation by saying, "We on Capitol Hill are powerless unless the people of God rally behind us at the grassroots level of every state."

Accommodation. By bending the gospel to fit the masses, we water down the message of the cross. Some religious groups insist on updating the Bible to match the times. God doesn't need *updates*; He wants people to *uphold* His Word. Those who want to accommodate the world instead of leading it argue we must loosen our standards and lighten up on commitment and holiness. Politically correct Christians want to be tolerant, open-minded, and nonjudgmental. But what we tolerate we cannot change. This is a day of great struggle, not a time to bow down to the enemy. We must advance God's kingdom!

We don't need to retreat from conflict or accommodate the masses. With God's strength you can stand up when others ridicule you, like Power Team member Berry Handley did one afternoon at the University of Oregon. Though his six-foot-seven, three-hundred-pound frame has earned him the nickname "Human Giant," that day he faced other giants. Berry looked out over a festive, somewhat barbaric campus. When the muscle-clad team came on stage, women whistled suggestive cat calls, several spectators passed strange-smelling substances, and a man dressed in a clown suit mockingly ripped a banana in half. Berry felt apprehensive about his role as that afternoon's keynote speaker. His emotions paralleled the spiritual battle taking place that day. A veteran campus pastor commented it was the biggest evangelistic event there in a century. However, omnipresent New Age philosophies left most area church leaders with a lack of expectancy.

Everything was set in place. Bricks were stacked high, steel bars ready to bend, hot water bottles waiting to be blown up, and baseball bats poised for snapping. The stage setup had drawn a huge crowd, including a mocker who printed a sign reading "Steroids will shrink your ———— and the Bible will shrink your mind." (Note: Every Power Team member is drug-tested and steroid-free.)

After the prankster paraded the sign around, provoking more mischief, Berry pointed and yelled, "Hey, you see this guy carrying the sign?" Pausing, he quoted 1 Corinthians 1:18, "For the word of the cross is to those who are perishing foolishness, but to us who are being saved it is the power of God." He continued, "Let me give you my paraphrased version: The message of the cross is a joke to guys like this, who are dying and going to hell, but to the Power Team it's the power to change us and save our souls!"

He spoke with such force and spiritual conviction his words melted the hostility. The crowd listened intently as he explained how every one of the team members had been freed from past chains like drugs, alcohol, feelings of hopelessness, or even anorexia. This was what the students needed to hear. That day some two hundred received Christ as their Savior. Meanwhile, the sign-carrier vanished into the recesses of the crowd. Berry Handley is a true champion and giant-killer in our generation.

We are entering a season where God needs giant-killers just like Berry who are prepared for the fight. Psalm 3:7 says, "For Thou hast smitten all my enemies on the cheek; thou hast shattered the teeth of the wicked." This is the kind of victory we need from God, so that we may remove the recognition and acclaim for evil from our nation.

Most people know the story of the great battle between David and Goliath. But not everyone realizes David's full intent. As he set out to meet the giant, the shepherd picked up five smooth stones (1 Sam. 17:40). Why five? It wasn't in case he missed the first throw. His probable motive appears in 2 Samuel 21:22: Goliath had four brothers. David wanted to wipe out the entire clan! Fighting giants has great significance. We are not trying to rid society of one ill. We must prepare for a clean sweep.

God is raising up a new breed of Davids today, giant-killers who will cut down Goliath and go after his four brothers. Don't be shocked when you see enemy forces mounting. We live in one of the darkest ages of history, but if you will hold your ground, God will intervene for you just as He did for David.

When others criticize you for daring to fight, will you respond like David, saying, "Is there not a cause?" (1 Sam. 17:29, KJV). Is there not a cause when homosexuality is taught as natural and normal, abortion on demand is legal, and pedophiles steal children from their homes? Is there not a cause when we see the media glorify abnormal behavior?

When students are killing their teachers in the classroom is there not a cause? When euthanasia is becoming an accepted method of ending life? When the theory of evolution is taught as fact and the Bible is taught as a fairy tale is there not a sound reason? When beer companies and drug dealers rape the destiny of this generation to feed their unbridled lust for money, is there not a cause? When our nation looks favorably on paganism and rejects the God who brought it to life is there not a God in heaven who will bring swift judgment on our nation if we refuse to repent?

What about in your personal life? Are you man enough to overthrow the forces that want to sidetrack you from reaching your destiny? Can you face your lust, anger, pride, selfishness, discouragement, doubt, and fear, and use God's Word to overcome them? I know you can! Break down the resistance with persistence. As 1 Corinthians 1:27 says, "God has chosen the weak things of the world to shame the things which are strong."

Adds Ed Cole, "God's methods are men. While men look for better methods, God looks for better men."[9] So, you want to kill some giants? You must realize the greater the victory the more costly the battle. In the words of General Dwight D. Eisenhower, "There are no victories at bargain prices."[10]

Read on to see how you can defeat the master of mediocrity.

Basic Training

- *Courageous heroes are ordinary men with extraordinary spirits.* It's not size, strength, or talent that matters, but the heart that lies beneath. A man obedient to God is to be feared.

- *Giant-killers rise above fear.* They will stake their reputation, finances, and lives to overthrow evil. (Prov. 29:25; Pss. 27:1; 118:6)

- *Faith will give you strength in the battle.* David's faith gave him the courage to slay giants. Our belief in God's ability, not our own, makes the difference.

- *God wants you to speak against evil.* It exists in your community, no matter how large or small. (Prov. 28:1)

128

- *God's Word will help you overcome.* It can help you defeat enemies like pride, lust, anger, selfishness, and discouragement. (John 8:51; 14:23;1 Cor. 1:18)

Gut Check

1. What is our mission as warriors? (See Eph. 5:8–17; 1 John 3:8b)

2. List some of the giants in the land that especially concern you. What can you do to educate yourself about them and combat them?

3. Does your church retreat from or accommodate sin in order to be socially acceptable or politically correct? If so, in a spirit of humility and love, what can you do to change this stance?

4. Look at your own life. Are there any personal habits, sins, or weaknesses that loom over you like a giant? Read James 5:16. Why should you confess these problems to your pastor, spiritual mentor, or men's small group?

5. How can sins and weaknesses that you cover up strip you of dignity, character, and manhood? (Pss. 7:11–12; 32:3–5)

10

BEATING THE MASTER
OF MEDIOCRITY

There's no such thing as coulda, shoulda, and woulda. If you shoulda and coulda, you woulda done it.

—*Pat Riley, NBA Coach*

The advertisement leaped from the sports page in bold letters: **Victor, the wrestling bear, never defeated. Will take on all challengers.** *Wow!* I thought. *Here's a chance to be somebody. Imagine the crowds cheering when I take on Victor at the Anaheim Convention Center's recreational vehicle show.* I grinned. *This is my ticket to fame! If I can take that bear, think of what the people will say. Hey, think of what my buddies will say.*

Grabbing my older brother, Crazy Eddie, I yelled, "Let's go!" First in line when the doors opened, we made a beeline for Victor's dressing room. Striding down the hall, I kept muttering to myself: "I can take him. I bench press 470 pounds. I can squat over 600 pounds. I can take him. I can do it." I relaxed a little when we reached the bear's quarters and his trainer showed us a cuddly looking creature curled up in his cage and nursing a bottle of Kool Aid.

"Shoot, he ain't so bad," I whispered to Eddie. I didn't know how my brother felt, but I was scared to death. But fear didn't interrupt my daydreams of victory or at least putting on a good show. "You sure you boys want to go through with this?" the trainer asked. After we nodded, he said, "OK, then, just sign on the dotted line." He thrust a paper at us. The heading on the release-of-liability form screamed, "In case of DEATH or injury." Shoot. My masculinity was on the line. I grabbed the pen and signed.

Wrestling a bear was only the latest in a string of escapades through which I tried to discover my identity. Throughout my formative years the world kept telling me to be someone else. I struggled mightily to get bigger biceps, to be more socially popular, and get more women and self-fulfillment. I did my best to dress right, look right, act right, and be cool enough for card-carrying status in the "in crowd." Ironically, I had no idea of what the apostle Paul meant when he said, "Act like men" (1 Cor. 16:13). It seemed that from childhood on up I couldn't measure up to Madison Avenue's advertising images or Hollywood's hero portraits. My insensitive friends offered few condolences to a chubby, uncoordinated geek. When they chose up sides on the playground, they always picked me near the end. Whether academics, the school orchestra, or sports, my life blared forth a single note: average. As I grew older, even my dreams were tainted by mediocrity. As my last year of college unfolded, I resigned myself to a modest future as an anonymous sales rep for some faceless, monolithic corporation.

The thought of a bland destiny seemed bleak and unfair. I had put forth the supreme effort to remedy my feelings of mediocrity. I enrolled at USC to attach myself to a prestigious university. Despite my lack of talent, I made the football team. I joined a socially acceptable fraternity. Though these subconscious attempts at status told people what I did, they revealed nothing of the real me. Wrestling a bear was part of my long, futile search for fame, recognition, and identity.

Soon after our visit to the dressing room, Eddie and I stood in line with four other men, awaiting our turn. I strategically retreated to the end, hoping the black Alaskan would get fatigued before reaching me. Wrong! Nor did the Victor in the ring remotely resemble the harmless little fuzzball I saw in his cage. When he stood up he was taller than

Shaquille O'Neal by nearly half a foot. This mountainous bear measured seven feet, four inches tall, and tipped the scales at 650 pounds. Thank goodness he had been declawed and muzzled!

In quick order Victor mauled, molested, and delighted in persecuting his first five victims. I chuckled quietly as he turned my older brother into Silly Putty—that is until Eddie's time was through and I was next. Shakily, I climbed into the ring. Momentarily sizing me up, Victor reared back on his hind legs and prepared to pounce. I surged forward. Suddenly it seemed every light in the convention center sputtered out.

I came to my senses with a repugnant odor filling my nostrils. It smelled worse than the USC locker room! I realized the lights hadn't burned out. The huge bear was smothering me in his furry chest. Somehow I hung on . . . and on. While Victor had whipped five opponents in ten minutes, I somehow stayed alive for nine. But with this mammoth teddy's weight resting on my shoulders, how much longer could I stand?

"Oh, well," I grimaced. "If I'm going down, I might as well try something." As Victor prepared to wipe the floor with my face, I reached desperately for his hind legs and twisted them with all my might. To the shock of three thousand spectators, the bear fell with a thud! My eyes turned into saucers. OK. I had just knocked down a bear. Now what? The only thing I could think of next was to grab Victor in a head lock. I twisted and grunted. He shook me off like a house fly. I tried again. Victor growled. "Let him up!" the trainer urged. "You're getting him mad."

Not wanting to taunt anyone twice my size, I obeyed. Big mistake. When he arose, a crushing blow from his paw made my nose feel like it had been rearranged on the back side of my skull as the blood gushed out. When he tossed me to the mat on my stomach, I realized this bear knew how to wrestle! Flipping me over, he had put me in a half nelson, bringing me face to face with my hot-breathed attacker. And believe me, Victor needed a lifetime supply of breath mints.

The bear hovered above me, drool splashing on my face. Suddenly, without warning, his foot-long tongue shot out of his muzzle and licked my head. Raucous laughter and hoots sounded from the audience. Even worse, I felt like a human hors d'oeuvre. Then it hit me. I had washed my hair that morning with a new honey-orange, herbal-essence shampoo. Victor thought I was an all-day sucker. When I climbed into the ring, I had been scared of him. Now I was just disgusted. I conceded the match and yelled, "Get him off me!"

Later, when I arrived home, smelling like a bear, my father said, "Well, Son, did you win?" Instead of answering, I stumbled toward the shower shaking my head. At the end of the hall, I glanced back and shrugged, "Naw. You might say I got licked."

Master of Mediocrity

Wrestling Victor brought me attention, but it didn't spur any real changes. I was still third-string in football and life, earning average grades and feeling despair over the giant void in my daily existence. Mediocrity plagued my soul. The saddest truth lay in the fact that God does not manufacture mediocre men. By turning my back on Him through ignorance and compromise I chose this status, which began as a slight infection and grew into a bubonic-sized plague.

Mediocrity is the 1990s American epidemic for individuals, the church, and our nation. This ought not to be, especially among Christians. We need to take heart from the stories throughout the Bible of people who climbed out of obscurity and into the Hall of Faith. Despite their character deficiencies, the Lord elevated them to positions of prominence, purpose, and prestige. God is the Master who delights in taking Mr. Average and transforming him into Mr. Extraordinary. His greatest warriors are ordinary people, as shown by the following list:

Person	Who They Were	What God Made
Moses	Inarticulate/social failure	Spokesman and leader
Gideon	Hiding from enemy	General
Shamgar	Plowman	Judge
Jeremiah	Boy	Prophet
Disciples	Fishermen/ tax collectors	Apostles
Smith Wigglesworth	Plumber	Miracle worker

133

However, if you're expecting to become a champion through strenuous workouts, studying for a doctorate, or striving for national acclaim, stop right now. Simply pray and ask God to use your life for His glory. Only when I turned my life over to Jesus did I find the power to rise above the world's sea of confusion and discover what it means to be a man. I saw that persevering over the long haul, following Jesus' path and being secure in my identity as a man of God, is always superior to being a flash in the pan.

God doesn't expect you to accomplish mighty feats through your power, but He does expect you to do your part. The parable of the talents in Matthew 25:14–30 shows how He despises lazy, mediocre men. Whiners moan about their deprived backgrounds, terrible fates, or crushing handicaps. Extraordinary men assume responsibility and shape their own destinies. Life may hand a godly man a lumpy mess of circumstances, but with God's power He sculpts triumph from the clay of tragedy. He'll turn your scars into stars! Men, you could have so much more if you would refuse to settle for less.

Hebrews 6:12 exhorts us to resist becoming mediocre Christians: "Then, knowing what lies ahead for you, you won't become bored with being a Christian, nor become spiritually dull and indifferent, but you will be anxious to follow the example of those who receive all that God has promised them because of their strong faith and patience" (TLB). I saw this truth in my own life. Through faith in Christ I rose above mediocrity in morals, manhood, career, destiny, and family life. Through Him I entered a lifetime of fulfillment and promise.

Mediocrity breeds insensitive husbands, distant dads, and apathetic church members. It often hides behind a macho-man image in which a man's fierce boasts are all illusion. Mediocre men come in all shapes and sizes. They may be monetary successes but moral failures, huge in physique but tiny in spirit. Though they roar like lions, underneath they are cowardly mewing kittens.

The mediocre-man epidemic spawned the modern-day feminist movement. Males' spiritual, emotional, social, and ethical lapses created a very negative view of men: "A Roper poll recently compared women's attitudes toward men today versus twenty years ago. . . . The results: 'American women see most men as lecherous, egotistical slobs. . . . The national poll found increasing numbers of women expressing annoyance at sexism and describing men as manipulative, oversexed, and mean.' Forty-two percent of women called men basically selfish and self-centered."[1]

Only through male Christian trendsetters can we erase these negative images. A single streak of mediocrity in a man of God can pollute every other virtue he possesses. Virtue is needed to produce men who willingly storm into battle and combat evil in our homes, culture, and nation. Bulldogs of faith will clamp the teeth of the gospel into evildoers. (Did you know a bulldog's nose is slanted backward so he can continue breathing without letting go?) That's how tenacious we must be as Jesus' warriors.

If you have the will and are prepared to fight, God will give you the victory in every area of your life. Best of all, God doesn't need multitudes to accomplish His tasks. Remember the story of Gideon? He started with an army of thirty-two thousand, but God whittled out the mediocre men until only three hundred loyal, courageous men remained (Judg. 7). This is the type of man you can be as Christ's warrior. While mediocre men hide, cast off self-restraint, and compromise their convictions, you can answer life's challenges with power and might. Don't fall prey to mediocrity; it ruins everything it touches.

Seven Symptoms of Mediocrity

Mediocrity has at least seven symptoms. I pray that exposing these habits will help you avoid mediocrity and search for ways to rise above it. You may know of other symptoms, but I believe these do the most damage to the body of Christ.

1. Irresponsibility. We live in an age of irresponsibility. We are told character does not count. A good example of this is seen in our political arena. Modern elections place more emphasis on sex appeal than character. Being understanding and sympathetic with the public is deemed of more value than standing up for just causes and speaking the truth. The *Boston Globe's* Mike Barnicle summed up the dilemma in this commentary angle:

Are they [politicians] liars? Chronic trimmers of the truth? Or merely . . . representatives of a widespread aspect of our culture, the growing inability to accept any personal responsibility for anything negative? Kids not doing well in school? Teachers' fault. Didn't get a raise or promotion? Boss hates you. Charged with a crime? Cops lie. Convicted of a felony? Lousy lawyer. . . . From courtrooms to kitchens to assembly lines, Americans work overtime to perfect the art of the excuse. It is the excuse that best serves ambition today. The excuse that enhances rather than harms reputation. The excuse that is far more marketable than the truth. And excuses are not necessarily lies; they are simply verbal detours around facts.[2]

We live in a culture that has mastered the art of excuses, justifications, and cover-ups of our mistakes. But men of God need to rise above that. Irresponsibility is no laughing matter. It stunts a man's growth and weakens his credibility for leadership. This sad state comes from ignorance of God's Word and His patterns and principles. First Corinthians 13:11 says, "When I was a child, I used to speak as a child, think as a child, reason as a child; when I became a man, I did away with childish things."

It is time to put away childish excuses. Claim responsibility for the conditions of your life. From personal habits at home to ethics at work to the convictions that govern your daily affairs, take inventory and stand accountable before God. If you have made errors, admit it; with the Lord, there is forgiveness and cleansing. Ask God to help you change. Remember, you'll never be responsible enough for success if you are not willing to be responsible for your failures.

2. Unreliability. Uncommitted, unreliable men search for loopholes, scapegoats, and the path of least resistance. Going with the flow is OK for rivers, but it leads to crooked people. Any dead, stinking fish can float downstream. Today's generation is full of men following the world's current, with dreams decaying through fear and apathy. Their lives are disasters waiting to happen.

What about you? Can you be trusted? Do you allow others to hold you accountable? Do you hold a steady job or jump from place to place with regular intervals of unemployment? Are you able to accept constructive criticism? Or do you blame circumstances, supervisors, or fellow employees for your shortcomings? If it is the latter, your problem might be staring back from the bathroom mirror.

If you are in school, do you carry tasks through to completion? Or is your education marred by regular lapses and interruptions? Frankly, most employers don't care as much about the grade you received as whether you completed the course. It is completion that adds the marks of credibility and dependability to your character.

What about your spiritual commitments? Are you accountable to your pastor or other mature Christians? Or do you flit from church to church like a bumble bee so you never take root and never let anyone see the real you? Are you consistent in your devotional life? Does God count you among those who diligently search His Word? Remember, He cares less about a man's talents than He does his faithfulness (2 Tim. 2:2). It's the faithful man who will be entrusted with God's pearls of wisdom and gracious promises.

3. Spiritual Dryness. Often I hear a man say, "I'm going through some dry times." If that is the case, work through it quickly because you are one step away from getting burned. Jesus warned of spiritual dryness as He was going to the cross. As He passed a group of women mourning His fate, He asked, "For if they do these things in the green tree, what will happen in the dry?" (Luke 23:31).

Dry trees attract fire like a magnet does nails. If you enter a dry season, don't provoke flames by treating your spiritual life casually. Christians who begin to treat Jesus casually often become casualties! King David suffered from a season of dryness and casualness. Though he conquered giants, his lapse into mediocrity brought devastation and misery. The trouble started when he grew tired and reasoned he had done enough: "Look at all I've done for Israel." When Israel's army marched out to battle, the king took a siesta. David stayed home when he should have been on the battlefield. Second Samuel 11 describes how that led him to see Uriah's wife, which led to a flare-up of his lust. When he followed his impulses, he had sex with another man's wife, Bathsheba. But instead of confessing that mistake, he made matters worse. (Ps. 32:3–4)

Bathsheba became pregnant, but David tried to lure Uriah back from battle so the child would appear to be Uriah's. When that failed, he sent an order to the commander to draw back in battle so Uriah would be killed. Now David was guilty of murder, as surely as if he had swung the sword himself. Not until the courageous prophet, Nathan, pointed out his guilt did the king admit his crime.

Mediocre men try the same tactics. But only God can bring lasting solutions and reinstate them to His plans. I am convinced that if David had refused to listen to Nathan, his usefulness to God would have ended. Yet because of his heart-felt repentance, the Lord revitalized him. In grateful response, David wrote, "It is a broken spirit you want—remorse and penitence. A broken and a contrite heart, O God, you will not ignore" (Ps. 51:17, TLB).

David laid in bed all day and then became distracted while lounging on the castle roof. What about you? Are you joking in the bars instead of going home? Are you staying at home on Sunday morning rather than attending church? Are you watching TV when your mate needs help with household chores? Are you going to professional ball-games with your buddies instead of helping your children with their homework or just giving them your time? You don't even have to be doing something wrong to neglect your duties. When you ignore responsibilities, a pattern develops. Dislocation leads to deception, which leads to destruction.

4. Inability to Handle Hardship. Society is full of men who don't want to carry their own load. Unfortunately, churches have an abundant supply of spiritual freeloaders, who feed off others' faith and expect them to spiritually nurture their wives and children. They hide from inconvenience, shrink from discomfort, and avoid service. Instead of relying on God's grace, mediocre men cringe at adversity and buckle under pressure.

One of the toughest trials of my life occurred more than a decade ago. This crossroads experience could have buried me. I had just finished a summer leadership training course at a Bible school in Florida. Anxious to return to the West Coast, my friend Al Manamtam and I decided to drive straight through. Lynn, a young woman we met there, asked if she could ride with us. About 3 A.M. we were two hours east of El Paso, Texas. My turn came to take the wheel.

138

Al and Lynn soon dozed off. With sleepiness tugging at me, I gradually ebbed away from consciousness. I awoke with a jolt when the car drifted off the highway and headed down an incline toward the median strip. Trying to jerk the wheel back onto the road, I turned it too sharply. Our compact car flipped head over tail half a dozen times. The only thing I remember is screaming, "Jesus, help us!"

When we stopped I looked around frantically. Next to me Al lay in his seat unconscious. Lynn was nowhere to be seen. Adrenaline pulsing through my veins, I leaped out the window and yelled for her. Finally I heard moaning and raced to the spot where she landed when she flew out of the rear hatchback window. Climbing up to the road surface, I waved frantically at the few cars zipping by in the pre-dawn hours. One stopped to help, but seeing my size and the blood must have scared the driver because he took off. Finally, a Christian truck driver radioed for help.

When they placed us in the ambulance, Lynn seemed to be stable. Al was telling a nurse about Jesus. Not long after we arrived at the hospital, though, a doctor came into the emergency room in tears. "We lost her, Son," he said. My heart sank. The only word I could mumble was, "How?" He replied that too much time had passed to repair the damage from her crushed lungs and internal bleeding. But the doctor went on to say that Lynn's death had moved him like none other: "I've seen babies die, old folks die, but never anyone like her. She just suddenly looked up with big, bright eyes and a radiant smile and said, 'Daddy, Daddy' and then slipped off."

If the shock of losing Lynn wasn't bad enough, Al had suffered a broken neck and was expected to be laid up for nine weeks. Though sick with grief and feeling the weight of responsibility crashing over me, I felt the Lord saying, "Son, get up and go on." Walking down the hall, I found an empty room and spoke to Satan as if he were standing in front of me.

"Devil, Lynn's dead. Al's hurt. But I want you to know you didn't get me, and I'm coming after you! Everywhere I go, whatever I do, every time I give an altar call, I'm going to make you wish you had never touched my friends. I'm going to kick your tail from one end of this globe to the other in remembrance of Lynn and win more souls for God than ever before. Satan, I will never back off from my commitment to destroy you!"

Though painful, this experience did the most to set my resolve for full-time ministry. It is still a motivating force. The events that followed strengthened me too. God did a miracle for Al and he got out of that hospital in just three days and returned home. Also some of the people at the hospital got saved.

Pressure and trials will come to everyone during their lifetime. How you respond determines whether you will be left with scars or stars. With God on your side you will always win. Don't be an escape artist when pressure comes. Hang in there!

5. *Fear of Failure.* Men who fear failure will never know the joy of success because they are too afraid to take risks. They will always fall short and live below God's standard. Businessman Jim Rohn says of failure, "We must all wage an intense, lifelong battle against the constant downward pull. If we relax, the bugs and the weeds of negativity will move into the garden and take away everything of value."[3]

If you live in fear of man, circumstances, or what God has called you to do, you are a spiritual babe. The apostle John reminds us that if we love and trust God we can't harbor fear because "there is no fear in love; but perfect love casts out fear" (1 John 4:18). Fear stems from not knowing God and keeping His Word. John also points out that "whoever keeps His word, in Him the love of God has truly been perfected" (1 John 2:5). The only way to battle fear is with more faith. Faith increases as you read and meditate on God's Word (Rom. 10:17).

6. *Stubborn Independence.* The man who flies solo cuts himself off from fellowship and valuable input into his life. He will eventually crash and burn. Yet the world glorifies everything from the super-action hero to the individualist who demands tailor-made hamburgers. The self-sufficient, independent man needs no one. Disposable relationships attract him because he is a user, concerned with benefiting self. Whenever the thrill wears off, the money runs out, or higher responsibilities threaten, he is gone like the wind.

Proverbs 18:1 accurately describes the independent man: "He who separates himself seeks his own desire, he quarrels against all sound wisdom." Do you know someone like that? No matter what you say, or how wrong he is, he refuses to look at another viewpoint. Such a man is guilty of idiocy. The root of this word comes from *id*, meaning "self" or "private person." He lives in the realm of his own imagination and doesn't have any viable relationships with anyone else.

Independent people won't put roots down in a local church. They spout empty reasons like, "I can follow the Lord's leading in my heart." But ignoring checks and balances that others provide leaves us walking on treacherous, shifting sands. God established His church as a place where relationships can be built and guidance obtained. None of us is wise enough to live without interaction and fellowship. Proverbs 24:6 advises, "In abundance of counselors there is victory."

God isn't looking for spiritual Lone Rangers. Christ isn't coming back for heroic individuals. He is returning for His bride—the church. The Bible constantly depicts Jesus as a shepherd guiding His flock and Satan as a wolf. A wolf on the prowl doesn't attack the shepherd or the whole flock. He picks off his victims one at a time: the weak, stragglers, rebellious drifters, the sick. Don't fall prey to the enemy through foolish, stubborn independence.

7. *Indecision and Compromise.* A mediocre man will live a life of regret because of instability and lost opportunities. Being double-minded, he constantly wavers between right and wrong, most often yielding to compromise and sin. James 1:8 calls the double-minded man "unstable in all his ways." Everything from his finances to home life are headed for self-destruction. God looks for men of firm conviction who, because they stand on the truth of His Word, are able to do great things. Isaiah 33:6 promises, "He shall be the stability of your times."

One sign of a man with conviction is the courage to share his faith publicly. Gene Waters, a UCLA football player, who came to a campus meeting in the spring of 1995, had never been in church, but the truth of the gospel hit him right between the eyes. Gene made a commitment to Christ, so genuine that he immediately left the party scene and began openly sharing his faith. Gene was the third of four offensive linemen to accept Christ in a short period of time. UCLA campus ministry director Gregg Tipton nicknamed them "The Heavenly Hogs."

Soon Gene started telling people in the weight room they needed Christ in their lives. One day some guys jokingly called him "The Prophet" and "Moses." Refusing to back down, Gene replied, "Hey, if I became half the man Moses was, I'd be honored." Later, as Gene walked out of the gym with one of the other Heavenly Hogs, he said, "Hey, Chad, who in the heck is Moses?"

You see, you don't have to be a Christian for twenty years or a sage seminary graduate to tell others about Jesus. The strong witness of the Heavenly Hogs has created a major impact at UCLA, and not just among their unsaved teammates. A group of "closet Christians" on the team found the courage to speak up. Gene told me, "There was like a private club in the locker room. No one ever knew who they were. But since we've been so vocal about our faith it has encouraged others to speak boldly in the name of Jesus. That's good. I refuse to live a half-hearted commitment."

Mediocre men shrink from public witnessing, but the righteous are as bold as lions—or should I say Heavenly Hogs?

Basic Training

- *Don't let the world define your identity.* You will never be happy trying to fulfill others' expectations. Let your identity be defined by God's Word!

- *God doesn't make mediocre men; they choose to be that way.* When you turn your back on Him, you settle for less than the best.

- *Men of courage accept responsibility.* They restrain their natural impulses and stand by their convictions.

- *You must be committed to carry out God's plans.* Otherwise, you will turn and run at the first sign of trouble.

- *Be a man—take a stand.* Courageous men share the story of their faith with others.

- *Casualness leads to casualties.*

Gut Check

1. What does the Bible say about mediocre men? (See Zeph. 1:12; Rev. 3:15–16.)

2. What are the pitfalls of mediocrity? (See Titus 1:15–16; James 1:8; 4:4.)

3. What failures did you experience in childhood? How did that make you feel? List some ways those failures are still holding you back.

4. Explain why (or why not) the list of biblical heroes on page 133 inspires you. Can you envision God transforming you into a great man?

5. How do you feel about so many women labeling men as selfish and self-centered? Is that an accurate statement? How do you intend to change that opinion?

6. Evaluate your commitment to Jesus Christ, your family, and your church. Go down the list of the seven symptoms of mediocrity and write down areas in which you need to mature. Note any correlating Scriptures to help you battle mediocrity, such as these Proverbs: 6:6–11; 10:4–5; 12:24; 15:19.

7. What symptoms of mediocrity do you struggle with? How did they become part of your life? Do you have the courage to admit it and ask God to help you change?

8. Are you afraid of failure?

11

COURAGE TO
ANSWER THE CALL

Leaders are like eagles. They don't flock, you find them one at a time.

—Anonymous

I admire Bill McCartney for the courageous stands he took at the University of Colorado, where he coached football for thirteen seasons. Besides lifting the Buffaloes from the dregs of college football to top-25 status, he withstood attacks that would have leveled a faint-hearted man. Highly misunderstood and persecuted by the news media and political activists for his biblically based beliefs (as he still is), he withstood the heat of confrontation and persecution and emerged a champion.

But my respect for him increased mightily after he shocked the sports world in November of 1994 by announcing his retirement at the height of his career. He has shared the story of this decision at many Promise Keepers rallies and in the updated version of his autobiography—how a message by famed evangelist Jack Taylor showed him he needed to dramatically alter his course: "'If you really want to know about a man,' he said, 'and if you want to know what kind of character he has, you need only look at the countenance of his wife.'. . . He concluded by saying that each of us is called by God to bring our wives to splendor in Jesus Christ. And it broke my heart to admit that I had not done that."[1]

I read with amusement the news coverage that greeted McCartney's announcement. Persons who had savagely ridiculed him for his stands against abortion and homosexuality and for the truth of Scripture suddenly praised him to the skies. Others smiled, shook their heads, and sneered, "He's just going to take a year off and then he'll go back to coach Michigan or some other major college team. You'll see."

I knew differently because of a brief telephone conversation after that press conference. Wanting to encourage him, I said, "Boy, what a blessing it will be to do more work heading up Promise Keepers now that your time will be freed up." A long pause let me know I had spoken presumptuously. "Tom, it's not like that for now," McCartney finally said. "All I know is that I need to give something back to my wife and minister to her needs and my family for now."

The second-guessers searched for ulterior motives. They theorized that McCartney was tired of the coaching grind, he couldn't handle the pressure, and on and on and on. Some probably doubted his manhood for supposedly caving in to his wife's demands. But the founder of Promise Keepers displayed the courage to answer the call. God showed him where he had made a mistake and he resolved to correct it.

Regardless of his future occupational role, he knew his first obligation was to set things right at home. The afternoon we talked, I sensed the spirit of the apostle Paul speaking from his heart: "Not that I have already obtained it, or have already become perfect, but I press on . . . forgetting what lies behind and reaching forward to what lies ahead" (Phil. 3:12–13).

Direction in Life

Do you have courage to answer God's call on your life? Or are you like the young men I hear on the radio station they air at my health club? They have an open-call show where women talk to men and ask questions like, "Well, tell me something about yourself. How big are your biceps? What kind of car do you drive? Where would we go on a date? What do you like to do?" This kind of superficiality is sickening enough. But what really baffles me is the men's frequent response, "Well, you know, I just like to hang out."

Just hang out? What an aimless existence! The truth is you don't have to be in your teens or twenties to "hang out." Plenty of men wander through life stopping by the bars, playing cards, watching TV, going to the big game, and taking vacations, which is about the only time they plan much further ahead than the weekend. They never teach their children morals and values that will sustain them through life or consider the legacy they will leave. Hanging out is a common way of life because it is easy. It makes few demands on your free time and presents no challenges. You can cruise all the way to the grave.

Years ago Ed Cole challenged me to consider my direction. One day as we were moving some furniture from his home, he said, "Tom, you've got to define your ministry. You've got to define your passion. What have you been called to do?" I gave him some brief, rather lame answers. He pressed me harder, scoffing, "That's no vision! Come on, let me hear something of substance. Who are you? What are you? What does your name stand for? What are you going to do in this world?"

That grilling hurt, but it forced me to face reality and decide what path I wanted to pursue. Dr. Cole urged me to clearly state my mission—sum up in one sentence what God was calling me to do. After researching various options, looking through the Scriptures, and much prayer, I finally got it—the Lord's mission statement for my life: "To train Christians to be leaders who will impact the world with the gospel of Jesus Christ." I also found a supporting Scripture: "And we proclaim Him, admonishing every man and teaching every man with all wisdom, that we may present every man complete in Christ. And for this purpose also I labor" (Col. 1:28–29).

During this time of reflection I began studying American history and found a great example of a man who carried out this lesson in Colossians. Reverend John Witherspoon (1723–94) trained dozens of great leaders in our formative Colonial era. Among his protégés were James Madison, who became the fourth president of the United States;

a vice-president; seventy congressmen; a host of future judges; Supreme Court justices; and other participants in the Constitutional Convention. A signer of the Declaration of Independence, Reverend Witherspoon also served as president of the College of New Jersey, which later became Princeton University.

Just one man, courageous enough to answer God's call, impacted the destiny of our nation. This is what matters, not having a well-known name, holding huge rallies, or speaking to crowds of admiring listeners. God's work is often done in intimate settings of prayer, Bible study, and small groups. Besides, you can't stand before crowds without first spending quiet time in the Lord's presence.

Strive to find your destiny and then answer it. A man who has a job and a purpose finds security and meaning. Those emasculated by aimlessness, welfare, drugs, or hopeless dreams sleepwalk through life. Finding your destiny doesn't mean you will know every detail of the future, but will lend you necessary direction. Recently, I saw the difference destiny and purpose make when I spoke at a summer camp to young men who had decided to seek God's vision for their lives. Many of these teens said, "Hey, I don't know exactly where I'm headed, but that doesn't matter anymore because I'm on the way. I'm on the right path and I know that it will be revealed to me."

You should have seen the looks of determination in those young men's faces! Because of the patterns and principles they had learned, their hope ignited fires of passion from within. That is what will keep them walking steadily on the Christian road, not the fear of going to hell or a dim hope of some day limping into heaven. The knowledge of God's call on their lives, and their ability to answer the call by God's grace, made them stand up with courage and conviction.

A Spine Is a Terrible Thing to Waste

Spiritual backbone is needed to step into manhood and not shrink from its challenges. God is looking for men who will determine to lead, who want to shake the world, and who want to positively influence our society by fulfilling God's dominion mandate, "making disciples of all nations." Faithful men will seize their destiny and pursue their calling with single-minded devotion. They will remember the truth outlined in Genesis 2:15: "Then the LORD God took the man and put him into the Garden of Eden to cultivate it and keep it." Knowledge of God's desire that men rule His creation gives them the determination to withstand life's tests of fire.

God commits to faithfulness, not talent. Sitting in church or some other Christian meeting and vowing that you will stand for God is easy. But if you are not faithful when you go back to your office, home, neighborhood, and marketplace, such bold statements are empty promises.

I know how tough it is to transfer willingness to action. As a young married man, I frequently failed to put my home on equal footing with my ministry. I met often with my pastor for counseling, but I had to reach a point of desperation before I was willing to change. Quitting the marriage would have been so easy—or settling for less than God's best: becoming like millions of couples who merely coexist instead of growing together and meeting each other's intimate emotional needs.

There were times I didn't know how I could work my way through the challenges of responsibility, communication, and intimacy, but through the power of the Holy Spirit Dana and I steadily gained victory after victory. It took courage to embrace change and allow God to mold my character. But as He taught us more about selflessness and the willingness to serve, our marriage began to grow and prosper. Gradually, I grasped the truth of Genesis 2:22—Dana was God's gift to me. He had brought her to me and I should be eternally grateful for her.

Likewise, God will provide you the strength and endurance to carry out His commands in all areas of life. But He frowns on those who are not committed and don't want to be faithful in their callings. Zephaniah 1:12 says, "And it will come about at that time that I will search Jerusalem with lamps, and I will punish the men who are stagnant in spirit, who say in their hearts, 'The LORD will not do good or evil.'"

Wrestling with Destiny

I enjoy playful wrestling matches with our son Stephen. Though I could squash him like a bug, I often let him win—but not without effort on his part. I gently hold him back and make him fight to see how badly he wants to win. I don't want to hurt him. I am trying to strengthen his muscles and develop his determination. The perseverance he learns on the living room carpet will serve him well later in life.

This is what Jacob learned in history's all-time championship wrestling match. The story is told in Genesis 32:24–30:

> Then Jacob was left alone, and a man wrestled with him until daybreak.
>
> And when he saw that he had not prevailed against him, he touched the socket of his thigh; so the socket of Jacob's thigh was dislocated while he wrestled with him.
>
> Then he said, "Let me go, for the dawn is breaking." But he said, "I will not let you go unless you bless me."
>
> So he said to him, "What is your name?"
>
> And he said, "Jacob."
>
> And he said, "Your name shall no longer be Jacob, but Israel; for you have striven with God and with men and have prevailed."
>
> Then Jacob asked him and said, "Please tell me your name." But he said, "Why is it that you ask my name?" And he blessed him there.
>
> So Jacob named the place Peniel, for he said, "I have seen God face to face, yet my life has been preserved."

This story concerns a man who had finally grown up. Jacob had received his father's blessing through deception; about twenty years later God decided to test him. Throughout his life, Jacob had gotten away with trickery so often it was his standard operating procedure. But now the Lord said, "I'm going to see how badly he wants to live for Me. How badly does he really want My blessing and to fulfill My purpose?"

For the first time in Jacob's life his clever, cunning ways failed him. He had nowhere to run. He couldn't make it on his father's faith or reputation. He couldn't hide behind his momma's skirts. He was alone in the desert. To make matters worse, his brother Esau—whom Jacob feared wanted to kill him for stealing Esau's blessing—was coming his way. Jacob had to stand on his own two feet, assume responsibility, and face God as a man. He had to wrestle for his destiny with the Almighty and grab hold of his calling. Then he had to answer the big question: *Could he live it?*

Don't mistake what happened. Jacob didn't body slam the Lord or give Him a Russian soufflé. God could have held him down with much stronger force than I use on our son. He could have effortlessly pinned Jacob for eternity. The Bible says the angel touched the socket of his hip and threw it out of joint. Now that's power! Just imagine if this was the World Wrestling Federation. Two seconds after the opening bell Jacob would have been tossed to the mat and laid there like overcooked spaghetti.

No wonder he walked with a limp from then on. Wrestling with God will dislocate self-made plans, dreams, and desires, and expose you to the Supreme Power. The mark of a real man of God is the one who walks with a spiritual limp. It proves he has been in the battle. Many Christians love to share testimonies about great triumphs, but the Lord gets more glory when you share your struggles. It reminds me of the meeting where Dennis Peacocke said, "I don't want to hear about your latest victory or greatest testimony. I just want to see your scars. I want to know that I'm talking to someone who's just been in a battle."

Now, Jacob wasn't the only one who was wrong in the past. His brother Esau despised his birthright, the covenant that belonged to him as the family's firstborn son. He sold it for some morsels of food when he was hungry. The world is desperate to see men who will wrestle for the covenant of God's blessings. Men on mission will purify the standards of this wicked world and preserve them for the next generation. Malachi 1:2–3 says, "Yet I have loved Jacob; but I have hated Esau." The reason God despised Esau is because he rejected his life's purpose. He didn't treasure the valuable covenant that was his for the claiming. Don't waste your life or despise your calling like Esau.

Likewise, men in today's generation sell out their future for ease and comfort. They complain it is too hard to find time for church. They forfeit their blessings so they can satisfy sexual lusts or materialistic cravings. They refuse to humble themselves to receive godly counsel.

If you want to answer God's call on your life, then you must pursue it with the same unyielding effort that drove Jacob to wrestle all night with the Almighty. You must desperately want the covenant that God promises to those who cling to Him. Maturity doesn't come with age but with striving to know the Lord, submission to the level of knowledge He has revealed to you, and acceptance of responsibility. Mature men, godly men, won't stop fighting until He gives them answers.

Soft Men

A second biblical figure provides another example of faithfulness and determination. Eleazar was one of three of David's mighty men who stayed with him to battle the Philistines when the rest of Israel's army had fled. Second Samuel 23:10 says, "He arose and struck the Philistines until his hand was weary and clung to the sword, and the LORD brought about a great victory that day; and the people returned after him only to strip the slain."

The Philistines were more than Israel's sworn enemy. They represent the world system that Christians face today. Eleazar walked into the middle of that system and took a stand. It didn't matter if everyone else disappeared. He took his sword in hand and started hacking at the enemy. He was desperate to see God's promises, so he was going to stand.

Are you that kind of man? Forget about swords, muscles, and wrestling matches. I'm talking about the sword of the Spirit, which is the Word of God. Do you crave reading your Bible daily? Do you want to do it so much that nothing can stop you? The day you turn your back on the Word is the day you begin slipping away from your destiny. Ignore the Bible and you will get swamped in the backwash of the world system, humanism, isolation, and the comfort of sinking into the sea of self-satisfaction.

You must pick up your spiritual sword and fight no matter how tired you feel. Only when Eleazar grew tired did the Lord step in and give him a great victory. You, too, may stand on the verge of one of the greatest victories in your life, but if you stop fighting you won't be able to claim it. Your destiny may be the very one the world is dying to see. So don't stop now!

The body of Christ needs strong men who are battle-tried and fire-hardened. Soldiers in God's army will keep their hand on the sword until it freezes there. Soft men will let go. The irony of "softies" is they have hard hearts. Instead of fighting for what they know is right, they make treaties with their flesh, the world, and Satan for the sake of peace and quiet. Such men exhibit six symptoms of hard-heartedness.[2]

Unwillingness to Face Hardship and Trial. They don't want to sacrifice or feel any pain. Jesus said in Luke 9:58, "The foxes have holes, and the birds of the air have nests, but the Son of Man has nowhere to lay His head." If our Lord didn't live in luxury, why should His followers expect it?

Lack of Self-Discipline. Everyone stumbles in this area. Never trying to improve is the problem. When my weight ballooned to 315 pounds, it represented a crisis. Not only was my fat, sloppy appearance endangering my health, it paralleled my spiritual life. I mentioned how John Jacobs goaded me to lose weight, but it wasn't just his (and other friends') words that reached me. God was speaking through His messengers. Self-discipline is also needed to overcome things like lust, anger, mediocrity, and double-mindedness. Remember, "He who rules his spirit is better than he who captures a city" (Prov. 16:32).

Resistance to Correction or Godly Counsel. I know people who make critical, life-changing decisions without prayer or outside counsel. After particularly bad choices, I'll ask, "Where did you come up with that?" They'll shrug and say, "Well, we just thought it was the Lord." If I ask, "Did you ask for confirmation? Did you talk with the pastor?" their snappy comeback is, "Well, we have other friends. You guys aren't the only ones who hear from God." The stubborn spirit behind such a statement shows they are going to cling to their ways even if their decision leads them down a disastrous path (Prov. 18:1).

Refusal to Face Reality. Not only does a soft man run away from tough decisions; he won't even admit he has needs. I know men whose homes have fallen apart, have just lost their jobs, are deeply in debt, and are wandering aimlessly. But when I ask how they're doing, they smile and respond, "Oh, fine. Just fine."

Development of Ties with Unbelievers. Worldly ties lead to lowering one's standards in order to be acceptable to others and adapt to their ways of living. This is why the Lord warned, "Do not be bound together with unbelievers; for what partnership have righteousness and lawlessness, or what fellowship has light with darkness? . . . 'therefore, come out from their midst and be separate,' says the Lord" (2 Cor. 6:14, 17).

Increasing Desire for Self-Gratification. Dozens of verses in the Bible refer to seed planting and harvest. The crops that emerge from the ground depend on the kind of seeds that are planted. The desires for self-fulfillment, self-pleasure, and self-glory grow from selfish seeds that take root in the heart and mind. This is why I constantly stress the need to be in the Word; as I like to say, "God's Word is mental floss to fight truth decay." Plant God's good seed in your spirit and you will bear such fruit as love, joy, peace, patience, kindness, and self-control.

Land of Milk and Honey

After years in the wilderness, Israel was finally ready to cross into the Promised Land of Canaan, a land described as flowing with milk and honey. Just as it took place thousands of years ago, I believe God has a land of milk and honey for you individually and for us as a nation.

God has a call on your life but He will never force you to respond. You must decide to seek it, find it, and answer it. That takes courage. As men answer their destinies individually, it will affect the entire country. Men pursuing God's vision for their lives will, in turn, bring vision to more than 250 million people. I believe it is a land of milk and honey when we dream about

- more Christians owning and operating businesses, including radio and television stations, and the positive implications that holds for improving public morality;

- families led by godly men who are raising up godly children, while also relieving the sting of divorce. As a society we like to shrug it off, but divorce has caused untold pain and suffering for millions of children, wreaked havoc on our social services system, and cost us billions of dollars;

- schools that are places of learning, discipline, and harmony, instead of battle zones requiring metal detectors, riot squads, and funeral wreaths for those who have lost their lives during classroom shootings.

What other positive developments would you like to see in your own community? Write them down, pray over this list, and ask God to help you bring them to pass.

Why is it important for you to seize the moment and answer God's call? The answer can be found by looking at Israel and the twelve spies who went to Canaan (Num. 13). Moses commissioned the representatives of Israel's twelve tribes. He commanded them to see what the land was like, gauge its population, and determine if they were weak or strong. Once there, the spies found the kind of harvest that would turn anyone's head, including a cluster of grapes so huge it took two men to carry it back on a pole.

However, there was a problem. Most of the spies thought the people were so big it would be impossible to overcome them, even though God had promised to give Israel the land. Only Joshua and Caleb insisted the Lord would give them the victory: "Then Caleb quieted the people before Moses, and said, 'We should by all means go up and take possession of it, for we shall surely overcome it.' But the men who had gone up with him said, 'We are not able to go up against the people, for they are too strong for us'" (Num. 13:30–31).

Those cries of doubt and faithlessness caused Israel to wander in the wilderness for a total of forty years and forfeit their destiny. During that time everyone over the age of twenty, except Joshua and Caleb, perished in the desert. What would it be worth to you to be one of only two men who saw God's promise fulfilled while multitudes around you died? Those are pretty steep odds. That alone should convince you of the seriousness of faith—and the consequences of disobedience.

The rewards were great for the two who refused to lower their standards when everyone else abandoned theirs. Two men stood and fought the good fight of faith while the rest murmured and complained. Two men clung desperately to God in spite of the overwhelming odds that stared them in the face. The names of two men, Joshua and Caleb, live on today while every doubter has disappeared into a sea of anonymity.

When everyone else is going the way of the world, are you willing to go the way of the cross? It isn't the road of ease and comfort, nor the course of least resistance. But I guarantee you it will be the most profitable. If you have been wrestling with your conscience over what you know God wants you to do, now is the time to surrender. He is calling. All you have to do is have the courage to answer.

Basic Training

- *Leaders stand above the crowd.* They don't wait and see what everyone else is doing before making their own decisions.
- *It takes courage to admit your mistakes.* Pride won't get in the way of a man who realizes he needs to correct his errors.
- *Establish a direction in life.* If you don't know where you're going, you will never get there.
- *Write a mission statement.* Sum up in one sentence what God has called you to do.
- *It takes a backbone to accept manhood's challenges.* Men who determine to influence society are the only ones who will.
- *Pursue God's call with unyielding effort.* Striving to know God takes courage, desire, and perseverance.

Gut Check

1. Courage to answer the call on your life starts in the home. What are you doing to make your home a haven of rest, peace, and security? Can members of your family talk to you about anything that concerns them, or are they afraid you may erupt like a volcano?

2. Re-read Philippians 3:12–13. How does "pressing on" apply to you? List three ways you plan to do that.

3. How is your mission going to make your community a better place in which to live?

4. Are you open to guidance and correction from others? Or are you afraid of what they will say?

5. How does your faith help you answer God's call? (Heb. 11:1–3, 6–11)

12

DON'T LEAVE HOME
WITHOUT IT

Men, in a word, must necessarily be controlled either by a power within them, or a power without them; either by the word of God, or by the strong arm of man; either by the Bible, or by the bayonet.
—*Robert Charles Winthrop, American legislator & author*

Reggie Jackson. Every baseball fan knows this member of the Hall of Fame. "Mr. October" ranks sixth on major league baseball's all-time home run list with 563; he earned his nickname for uncanny clutch hitting during the World Series. Reggie led his teams to five championships in the 1970s, three in Oakland and two in New York. At the end of his long major league career he joined the California Angels, who play near my home. I'll never forget his comment when a reporter asked about his superstar status: "Yeah, I guess I am a superstar by most people's standards of greatness. But that's just because most people are lazy."

Unfortunately, there are plenty of lazy Christians who won't take the time to strengthen themselves in the basics of life, which are found in the Bible. Celebrity spokesman Karl Malden became well-known over the years for his trademark line in the credit-card commercial that concluded, "Don't leave home without it." In our walk with God, security doesn't come by carrying a piece of plastic but from knowing the Book of promises and wisdom. The Word of God is the center of our devotion and the foundation of a lifestyle in Christ.

Evidence of our departure from the Word as the indispensable moral compass in our land is seen in countless ways, none as silly as the notion of "safe sex" that many have embraced, including spiritually cold churches. Speaking out against it is an invitation to be ridiculed. My pastor, Phil Bonasso, has received harsh criticism for his strong biblical views on dating and holiness. After all, they don't line up with the idea that you can play with fire and expect a pitifully thin condom to keep you from getting burned. But Phil never wavers from upholding virtue. Whenever others attack, he smiles and says, "I'm just a mere Christian, obeying Jesus and living up to the standards found in the Bible."

If you think those who quote Scripture and praise the Lord are fanatics, maybe you should examine your heart. It might be harder than a brick wall. Are you so wrapped up in your own desires and daily cares that God's Spirit can't penetrate your insensitive exterior? Take the advice of Jeremiah 4:3–4, "Break up your fallow ground and do not sow among thorns. Circumcise yourselves to the LORD and remove the foreskins of your heart."

Only a heart softened—broken of pride and selfishness—by God can receive His treasures, gems that won't rust, fall apart, break down, or disappear. If you knew all that the Lord has in store for your life, you would give up everything you own to find it. This is the picture outlined in Matthew 13:44–45: "The kingdom of heaven is like a treasure hidden in the field, which a man found and hid; and from joy over it he goes and sells all that he has, and buys that field. Again, the kingdom of heaven is like a merchant seeking fine pearls, and upon finding one pearl of great value, he went and sold all that he had, and bought it."

Precious Pearls

As a kid I collected thousands of baseball cards, eventually gathering some from as far back as the 1940s. I didn't know they would be worth something one day; I just liked having cards and daydreaming about these great players.

Years later, I decided to sell a few and invited a collector to look through them. When he got to a 1969 rookie card of Johnny Bench, his eyes lit up. We started talking about its value, and the longer we talked the more money he offered me. He was determined to have it. He started at twenty-five dollars, and when he reached sixty, I accepted his offer. To him, it was a pearl of great price.

So was a baseball when my brother and I were in our early teens and we went to the Angels' spring training in Palm Springs. No sooner had we reached the park than a "crack" sounded and a foul ball sailed toward us. The last thing I saw was Eddie diving into a pile of grown men. Soon, out he popped with the baseball. Instead of gleaming, it had deep cuts. When I asked how that happened, he wiggled his fingers in my face, grinned, and said, "Fingernails." He had dug into that ball so tightly nobody could grab it from him. Are you that desperate to hold on to God? Then you must be that desperate to hold on to His Word.

The world gets excited about cards, sports, coins, and CDs. Are we just as fervent in our search for life's true riches in the Bible? Did you ever hear how banks train tellers to recognize counterfeit money? They don't use fake bills; instead, they repeatedly show them real currency. When a phony bill passes over the counter, they can spot it instantly because they have been trained to recognize the genuine item.

Likewise, you won't know His truths unless your eyes are trained to find heavenly values in the Scriptures. Remember the lesson of Romans 14:17, which says, "For the kingdom of God is not eating and drinking, but righteousness and peace and joy in the Holy Spirit." In other words, you will find God's treasures in your Bible and prayer times, not on a luxury cruise ship, in a department store, or over the home-shopping channel.

Why desire these precious pearls? You will never become the great leader God wants you to be unless you decide to doggedly seek His wisdom and understanding through His Word. This is what makes you spiritually rich, mentally alert, and emotionally secure. Many will find the price too great or the labor too long. Their lust for money, glory, fame, power, and self-satisfaction will overcome their good intentions of living for God. Seduced by what the world values, some will be afraid of mockery or ridicule and fall for shallow, cheap imitations.

A desire to live up to God's standards doesn't mean that we, as believers in Christ, think we are better than anyone else. Like all weak, sinful human beings, on our own we fall short of the mark. But that doesn't mean the standard is worthless. It is something to aim at and when we give our best, God picks up the slack and pushes us over the top, making us more than victorious!

As we walk with Christ daily we mature and grow. Apart from His Word, this is impossible, because "Thy word I have treasured in my heart, that I may not sin against Thee. I shall run the way of Thy commandments, for Thou wilt enlarge my heart. Thy word is a lamp to my feet, and a light to my path" (Ps. 119:11, 32, 105).

When personal change is needed, the Word causes us to let Christ's lordship penetrate to new depths of our heart. God keeps raising the standard of His Word over our lives, saying, "How badly do you want it?"—namely, His friendship, our destiny, and other spiritual riches. You have to continually pay the price.

Razor-Sharp Sword

There are many wonderful translations of the Bible. Yet it is most effective when the Word comes alive through believers' actions. Other books are profitable for instruction, but God gave us the Bible for instruction *and* transformation. When we heed it as individuals and as a society, its power will revolutionize our world. Are you ready to use it and become a spiritual agent of power in the midst of darkness? The Bible is the primary tool of sweeping changes. This medicinal remedy for sin-sick souls carries the seeds of reformation by which evil empires fall.

The Word of God is a weapon of war. Hebrews 4:12 says God's Word is "living and active and sharper than any two-edged sword." This razor-sharp instrument brings judgment, redirecting those who study it and condemning those who ignore it. The apostle Paul admonished his spiritual son, Timothy, "Be diligent to present yourself approved to God as a workman who does not need to be ashamed, handling accurately the word of truth" (2 Tim. 2:15).

I didn't intend in this book to tell you how to get your life right with God, but how to take action for Him. Jesus wants His warriors to graduate from nursery school and stand with the heroes "who by faith conquered kingdoms, performed acts of righteousness, obtained promises, shut the mouths of lions, quenched the power of fire, escaped the edge of the sword, from weakness were made strong, became mighty in war, put foreign armies to flight" (Heb. 11:33–34).

Now, the gospel message doesn't come in mere words from men, but in power from God (1 Thess. 1:5). When we speak, stand on, or implement biblical ways, it is like brandishing a heavenly sword that demands obedience, submission, or change. This is why we need men who will boldly proclaim the truth of God's Word in our political, educational, and cultural centers.

Ignoring God's Word stirs His righteous anger. It brought His wrath on Moses' generation and the same neglect is brewing it again in our generation. "Therefore I was angry with this generation, and said, 'They always go astray in their heart; and they did not know My ways'" (Heb. 3:10). Negligence of God's Word and failing to walk in His ways will always harden the human heart with the deceitfulness of sin.

What soldier goes into battle without a plan or a weapon? If he storms in unprepared, he will come home in a body bag! By necessity, a soldier becomes intimately acquainted with his weapon. He is trained to use his gun in adverse circumstances and knows it so well he can assemble it in the dark. So should the disciple of Christ know the Word. We can all imitate Eleazar, whom I mentioned in the previous chapter. We should be so zealous for the sword of the Spirit that our hands freeze to the Word until we see God's victory.

Our very lives depend on letting the Bible nurture and build up our spirits. As a man meets with God privately and meditates on His Word, the results of these encounters will surface in public. His thoughts, words, and actions will be dictated by God's Holy Spirit instead of human reasoning or emotions. When a man keeps a daily date with God, his life becomes ordered, his wife and family are secure, and his community is dramatically affected by his godly example.

Christian warrior, if you want to get into the game, start by picking up your sword. You can't try sudden experiments when moments of crisis, difficulty, or great challenges arise. John Lowe, a sports writer for the *Detroit Free Press,* once told me, "You know what a miracle is? When preparation meets opportunity." We are to "be ready in season and out of season" (2 Tim. 4:2). Being ready means staying in the presence of God and listening to His words. When you are called, you won't hesitate to run into battle; you will have been waiting for the opportunity.

Making a Difference

One man can make a difference! I will never forget the tremendously moving story of Marine Lieutenant Clebe McClary, a soldier who displayed unbelievable courage during the Vietnam War. Even if you're familiar with it, I hope as you read this account you will envision the spirit of a warrior and draw encouragement for your Christian battles:

On my 19th and longest "recon" patrol in Vietnam, we went into a valley where very few of our troops had been. We sat on top of a hill and I had three men dig a foxhole to my right; my doc and my radio men were in a foxhole to my left. I got in a punji pit that I had cleared and put eight of my men around the edges of a large bomb crater about fifty meters behind me. It was about midnight when I thought I heard enemy movement. I crawled out of the punji pit to check if the men on the right had heard it.

Before I got to them a grenade came in from the side of the hill. It exploded, hitting me in the neck and in the shoulder.

As I grabbed the radio and started calling for air support and artillery, a Sapa unit, better known as a Suicide Squad, of about ten of the enemy started running up the hill. With grenades tied around their waists and grenades in each hand, they were coming up the hill just exploding, throwing grenades.

I shot a man right in front of me and he fell into the punji with me. He had a satchel charge in his hand which exploded, blowing both of us out of the hole.

As I was going through the air all I could think of was, "Man, where's my shotgun?" As I reached back for it, I realized my left arm had been blown off by a blast. I looked to my left. My radio man and my corpsman were dead or unconscious. Then I heard the three men on the right cry out and discovered that a grenade had gone into the foxhole. But a black Marine, Pfc. Ralph Johnson, had smothered it and there gave his life to save the other two with him. I started crawling toward them and before I got there another grenade came in. I threw up my right hand, the explosion blew out my left eye. My teeth on the left side were out, and I had lost a good bit of the use of my right hand.

Things were looking tough and I thought my only chance was to get back to the bomb crater where the eight men were fighting. I tried running, but a couple of grenades knocked me down.

I lay there for what seemed like hours. I had never wanted to live so badly in my life. If I could only see my wife one more time!

Later I heard some movement in the bushes behind me. One of the enemy came up and shot me in the right arm. Another stuck an NVA flag up about fifteen feet from my head. I thought it was all over. Then I heard a voice call, "Lieutenant! Lieutenant!" It was an eighteen-year-old Marine from Alaska. He crouched down by my feet and picked the enemy off just as they were coming up the hill. At the same time, Corporal Lucas, who had already won a Silver Star in Vietnam, crawled out of the bomb crater and also was returning fire. I said, "Luke, take over. Try to get helicopters to come in after us."

He radioed for choppers but they said they wouldn't come until daylight. I told him, "Tell them to forget it. We won't be here at daylight. We're out of grenades and throwing rocks."

He relayed this to the chopper pilots and instead of waiting, they came right in. It was just 3:00 A.M. when they put my two dead men, the four wounded and me on the first bird. As it lifted, the second helicopter landed. The last seven men dropped their packs—weapons, everything—and jumped on. As it lifted off about 150 of the enemy swarmed over the top of the hill. In a few more minutes not one person would have gotten off that hill alive.

Lord, give us soldiers for Christ with the same heart that was in Clebe McClary. Raise up laborers to go into your harvest. In Jesus' name, amen.[1]

I love hearing about the Clebe McClarys of this world. Despite his war wounds, McClary travels extensively (often with his wife, Deanna) to speak at churches, prisons, schools, prayer breakfasts, and motivational seminars. He wrote a book on his Vietnam experience titled *Living Proof,* which discusses his determination to press on despite the odds. Gospel Films also made a movie about his life titled *Portrait of an American Hero.*

The desperate hunger to live, yet give all he had for a cause, is the type of drive needed to be like Clebe McClary, a spiritual warrior for Jesus Christ. And to do God's works and walk in His blessings, a man must be desperate to meet Him daily in His Word.

Spending Time with God

Every day that you choose to spend time with God in His Word—not a minute or two, but at least half an hour—you are making a mark on your society. Do you know the truths of the Bible well enough to respond immediately to false teachings? Can God call on you on short notice to be His witness or will He catch you flat-footed?

I met recently with the director of a campus ministry who marveled at how many young believers couldn't properly defend their faith. "Tom, the false religions like Mormonism and the Jehovah's Witnesses put our kids to shame," he said. "They know their false doctrine like the back of their hand. But we Christians have the truth and we don't know it well enough to support it!" As this man asked, "What good is God's Word if we will not study to show ourselves approved as believers?"

Our faith is worthless if we can't back it up by logical reasoning from God's Word. Just carrying a Bible and telling everyone that you're a Christian won't help a bit unless you read it and put its words into action! Why should followers of Christ expect the world to respect a Book they so often neglect? While the world decays at an alarming rate, God needs men who won't make excuses about lack of time and will bring the living water of the Word to thirsty, dying people.

Speaking out won't always be pretty, but if God's Word is hidden in your heart it will come out naturally. I remember the time I walked into a 7-Eleven store with Stephen and Tommy. I wanted a can of soda, not a fight. Suddenly a boisterous woman barged through the door using the most vile language I have heard since the locker room in college. Her violation of my conscience and disrespect for my sons stirred a righteous anger inside me. When she boldly cut in front of us with her hamburger and a beer, I said sweetly, "Excuse me, ma'am. Are you really going to eat out of the mouth you're talking with? It's so filthy and dirty you might catch an infection or something." Seeing my boys, she ducked her head in shame and whispered, "I'm sorry."

Now, I didn't lead that woman to salvation, but I let everyone in that store—especially my sons—know that we didn't have to tolerate that kind of ungodliness. I praise God I was ready when an opportunity arose, instead of fumbling for words or remaining silent because of the fear of not knowing what to say. I was ready because I had been with Jesus. He wants His children to get into the game and contribute to the team's (the church) victory.

When used by His children, God's Word has amazing power. "The whole Bible was given to us by inspiration from God and is useful to teach us what is true and to make us realize what is wrong in our lives; it straightens us out and helps us do what is right. It is God's way of making us well prepared at every point, fully equipped to do good to everyone" (2 Tim. 3:16–17, TLB). God speaks to His children through His Word—Jesus said in John 10:27, "My sheep hear My voice." God will speak to you in many ways, but the foundation is always His Word. He will never contradict it. The ways He does this are outlined in the book *Experiencing God:*

> When the Holy Spirit reveals a spiritual truth from the Word of God, He is personally relating to your life. That is an encounter with God. The sequence is this:
>
> 1. You read the Word of God—the Bible.
> 2. The Spirit of Truth takes the Word of God and reveals truth.
> 3. You adjust your life to the truth of God.
> 4. You obey Him.
> 5. God works in and through you to accomplish His purposes.[2]

While it is essential to spend time in the word and prayer each day, the next step is to be willing to come out of our prayer closets and get dirty. Football players suffer embarrassment if they finish a game and walk to the showers still wearing a sparkling clean uniform. There is no glory in coming through a battle with no dirt, blood, or bruises.

I remember the high school game when I didn't get in for a single snap from scrimmage. Discomfort washed over me when I realized the cheerleader I liked would see me without a speck of dirt on my body. So right before we walked by her I reached down, grabbed a gob of mud, and smeared it all over the front of my uniform. I looked a little better, but I was still humiliated. Likewise, I wonder how many men will stand before God one day, realizing they led good, clean lives, but outside their personal existence made little impact in furthering His kingdom. I believe such men will experience incredible shame for missing out on the opportunities Christ sent their way.

Righteous Judgment

God sent us into the world to render judgment by upholding the light of His Word in every area of society. Don't fall for that humanistic line that unbelievers hide behind, namely that "we should not judge." They are taking a truth from Matthew 7:1 but lifting it out of context. The Bible says we are to judge with a righteous judgment. The key appears in John 5:30: "I can do nothing on My own initiative. As I hear, I judge; and My judgment is just, because I do not seek My own will, but the will of Him who sent Me." As children of light, we are commanded to expose darkness (Eph. 5:11). However, to do that we must be walking in obedience to His Word.

A. C. Green told me about a run-in he had with an NBA superstar. This player has what can be kindly termed "verbal diarrhea." When A. C. tried to correct the man about his bad speech, he stammered, "But . . . but . . . Ace, doesn't the Bible say, 'Judge not'?" Green started laughing and said, "Why is it that every sinner knows that one verse?" That superstar should have read all of Matthew 7:1–5, which warns about being a hypocrite but points out that those who are walking clean before God are called to pluck specks of evil out of our society.

Like that NBA star, those who pursue immorality cry, "You're judging me!" when someone tells them they are doing wrong. That isn't true. Christians have a duty to say what the Word says; the Word does the judging. You can't proclaim the Word if you remain a babe in Christ, though. God exhorts us in 2 Timothy 4:2 to "preach the word . . . reprove, rebuke, exhort, with great patience and instruction." This is our responsibility as soldiers of the cross.

Remember that soldiers not only preach but also act. When God makes something clear to you, you have the obligation to move. This is what drugstore magnate Jack Eckerd discovered after he met Charles Colson. Through Colson's persistent witness, Eckerd was born again. Later, as the reality of his decision took form, the founder of the Eckerd Drug chain acted. He removed *Playboy* and *Penthouse* from 1,700 stores, even though that decision cost his company three million dollars a year.

You may not manage a multi-million-dollar corporation, but the battles in your corner of the world are just as tough, as real, and as significant. There are no trial runs, controlled scrimmages, or test markets. The war over immorality that threatens our nation's future is one of immense proportions that will affect untold future generations. With God's Word in your heart there is nothing that you cannot do! Pick up your sword and fight: "Rair Simonyan of the Soviet Army said this about men and weapons: 'The most important thing is the man who is using the weapons. It doesn't matter what the weapons are, assuming he knows how to use the weapons and is well trained. The soldier or officer who will win is the one who thoroughly understands the goals of the war, who is striving to achieve those goals, and who is ready to sacrifice his life in the name of those goals.'"[3]

Burn Your Bridges

Are you sold out to Christ's Great Commission? Do you vow to uphold His Word in your sphere of influence? Have you burned the bridges of sin, compromise, and other escape routes behind you so that you can only look forward to Christ's calling and destiny? Then welcome to the fight. Be assured that it will be a good one. Let it be said of you as it was of the apostle Paul, "But I do not consider my life of any account as dear to myself, in order that I may finish my course, and the ministry which I received from the Lord Jesus, to testify solemnly of the gospel of the grace of God" (Acts 20:24).

Though the great Spanish explorer Hernando Cortez (1485–1547) conquered Mexico, in recent years he has come under attack from historical revisionists. They accuse him of exporting imperialism and attacking the poor, innocent Aztec Indians. In truth, Cortez performed a great service by freeing those who lived under the brutal Aztec regime. When he arrived in Mexico, he ordered his ships sunk in the harbor. Thus, his force of five hundred men realized they had to either triumph or die:

> Cortez came to free a nation from barbaric pagan cannibalism. His troops soon met with one horrendous sight after another: human hearts that had been cut out of living prisoners found nailed to temple walls; pyramid style temples covered with human blood; bodies of men and boys without arms or legs; human skulls stacked on poles; hundreds of thousands of human skulls regularly arranged in piles; gnawed human bones piled in houses and streets; wooden houses built with gratings jammed full of captives being fattened up for sacrifice; pagan priests matted with dried human blood, covered with the stench of carrion, practicing sodomy; humans sacrificed on pagan altars and then rolled down temple steps where frenzied hoards ate their bodies. . . .
>
> All this was a result of their religion, which believed that all the universe was one and that people were just a part of the universe. They believed that the Sun god needed human blood to live and that the Aztecs were responsible to feed him the blood that he needed daily.
>
> As the Spanish troops went from town to town, the Indian tribes were elated that they would be set free from the Aztec rule. Cortez would immediately free the captives awaiting sacrifice, break the idols, roll them down the temple steps, then erect a cross and preach Christ unto them.[4]

When these Spanish soldiers looked back to see their ships burning and no escape routes left, all thoughts of returning to their old world evaporated. So it is today for those who have accepted Jesus as their Lord and Savior. If you have come out of the world, burn your bridges (or sink your ships) and forget about ever going back. The only direction left is forward. Press on and fight for the dominion of Christ's kingdom. When the pressure is on and the battle rages, stand on God's Word. Then you, too, will stand victorious, beside the mighty King known as the Ultimate Warrior.

Basic Training

- *Spiritual maturity comes with a price.* If you're too lazy to study the Bible, then you will never have giant-sized faith.

- *Seek real treasures in life.* You must search the Bible with the same kind of zeal you would use searching for gold buried in your back yard.

- *You don't have to be perfect to follow God's standards.* Aiming for the best will lift you higher than shooting for the sewer.

- *The Bible is the tool of sweeping change.* Its words heal sin-sick societies and restore them to spiritual health.

- *Faith and the Word go hand in hand.* You must respect the Bible and know it if you expect others to want to follow it.

- *One man can make a huge difference.* The results of heroic actions will often only be appreciated in retrospect.

- *With God's Word in your heart there is nothing you can't do.*

Gut Check

1. What is the supreme test of your love for God? (See John 14:15, 23–24.)

2. Describe the kind of heart it takes to produce the "good fruit" of the Holy Spirit. (Luke 8:15)

3. Do you have a daily devotional time with Jesus? Read Mark 14:37–38. What should you be doing?

4. According to Hosea 4:6, why do God's people perish?

5. Look at 1 Thessalonians 1:5. Does your life give any evidence of the Holy Spirit's power?

6. How are you preparing to answer opportunity's call? (Ps. 37:3–11)

7. When we talk about seizing our destiny and fighting the good fight of faith, how does faith play a part? (See Rom. 10:17.) Is it enough to just hear the Word? (See James 1:22.)

8. How well can you explain and defend your faith? (Jude 3) Have you burned your bridges to the world so you won't be tempted to go back? (2 Cor. 6:14–18)

Epilogue

DEFENDERS
OF THE FAITH

The world is not moved or impressed with Christian air-heads.
—Tom Sirotnak

W hen true-hearted Christians talk about Jesus Christ and propagate the gospel to a very skeptical and unbelieving world, do they really underscore the deity of Jesus Christ? Do Christians really have the knowledge and believe that Jesus Christ is, in fact, God?

The essentials of historic Christian faith hinge on this one unalterable fact. There is one God (Deut. 6:4; Isa. 43:10–12; 1 Cor. 8:4; Gal. 3:20), and in this one God resides three persons, God the Father (Matt. 6:9), God the Son (Heb. 1:8), and God the Holy Spirit (Acts 5:3–4). Wherefore, God the Son (Jesus Christ) paid our wages of sin via physical death on a cross (Col. 1:20–22) and the power of the Holy Spirit raised Him (Rom. 8:11; 1 Pet. 3:18) to physical life on the third day (Luke 24:7; John 2:19–22).

Jesus had asked His disciples concerning Himself, "Who do men say I am?" (Matt. 16:13) and Peter, with a lightning-flash response, answered, "You are the Christ the Son of the Living God."

If Jesus were to ask most modern-day Christians, "Who do you say that I am?" could they affirm without a shred of doubt the true identity of Jesus Christ and prove it in the light of Scriptures? Did Jesus make claims to be divine, the Almighty, the second person of a triune God? Mormons and Jehovah's Witnesses peddling their convoluted theology door to door could turn the average Christian into a doctrinal pretzel on this issue.

Too many Christians are not prepared to combat the arguments against the deity of Jesus Christ. All of us as Christians should always be prepared to give an answer to everyone who asks us, to give a reason for the hope we have (1 Pet. 3:15). We should be prepared in season and out of season to preach the Word (2 Tim. 4:2).

The fact is, Jesus Christ did claim to be Jehovah God. The apostle Paul informs us that in Christ all the fullness of God Himself is in human flesh (Col. 2:9). For God was pleased to have all His fullness dwell in Christ (Col. 1:19). Paul understood with crystal clarity that Jesus Christ was the great God and Savior (Titus 2:13). The disciple whom Jesus loved (i.e., John, the apostle) confirms the Word (Jesus was in fact, God [John 1:1]).

After the resurrection, Jesus appeared to Thomas, the doubting disciple. Thomas saw the nail marks in Christ's hands and the hole in His side and was overjoyed with utter amazement. He said to Jesus, "My Lord and My God" (John 20:28). As a rabbi, Jesus would have rebuked Thomas for calling Him God, which would have been blasphemous; but as God, Jesus accepted it. Jesus said to Thomas, "Blessed are those who have not seen and yet have believed" (John 20:29).

One of the clearest affirmations of deity made by Jesus is in John 8, where Jesus had dialogue with nonbelieving Jews. Jesus spoke of Abraham, saying, "Your father Abraham rejoiced to see My day; and he saw it, and was glad" (v. 56). The Jews scorned Jesus for claiming that He saw Abraham. Thereafter, Jesus made this powerful affirmation, "Truly, truly, I say to you, before Abraham was born, I AM" (v. 58). To the Jews, the phrase "I AM" was a name of Jehovah the almighty God (Exod. 3:14).

Jesus had taken the divine name of God, "I AM," and applied it to Himself. Hence, He was claiming to be God Almighty, the One who spoke to Moses in the burning bush. The Jews wanted to kill Him for claiming He was God (John 8:59).

When Jesus claimed to be the "I AM" in John 18:6, it had caused the mob to draw back and fall to the ground. Jesus makes it super clear that salvation is dependent on the belief that He is God Almighty. In John 8:24, Jesus enunciated this: "You will die in your sins if you do not believe that 'I AM.'"

While under heated interrogation from the high priest, Jesus was asked if He was the Christ, the Son of God. Jesus answered, "I AM; and you shall see the Son of Man sitting at the right hand of Power, and coming with the clouds of heaven." The priest recognized the term "I AM" as a claim to deity. He was outraged and tore his clothes and said to the people, "You have heard the blasphemy!" (See Mark 14:61–64.)

Jesus claimed that He and the Father are one (John 10:30). After which, the Jews wanted to stone Him for claiming to be God (John 10:33). In John 5:17–18 the Jews understood that He was making Himself equal with God, and they sought to kill Him. Jesus told the people that in seeing Him they were seeing God (John 14:9). In knowing Him, they were knowing God (John 8:19). In believing Him, they were believing God (John 12:44). In honoring Him, they were honoring God (John 5:23). Jesus forgave sins (John 7:47–49). The Jews knew that only God forgave sin. Jesus received worship (Matt. 8:2; 14:33; 28:9; and John 9:38). In Hebrews 1:6, God the Father tells all the angels of heaven to worship Jesus. Yet in Luke 4:8 Jesus tells Satan, "Worship . . . God only."

Jesus proclaimed, "I am the First and the Last, the Alpha and the Omega" (Rev. 22:13). Wherein, God Almighty tells us in Isaiah 44:6, "I am the First and the Last. Besides me there is no other God." Since it is a linguistical error to have two firsts and two lasts, the Bible is proclaiming Jesus and the Father are one.

As Christians we must be aggressively sure of the essentials of historical Christian faith. We must be equipped to communicate what we believe and why we believe in a clear and cogent fashion, always contending for the faith that was once for all time delivered to the saints

(Jude 3). The whole world is under the sway of Satan and his cascade of demonic cohorts. To fight the good fight of faith, we must wear the armor of God tightly fitted, with sword in hand, swinging at all times. Our best defense is Scripture and having knowledge of the true God and Savior Jesus Christ. Jesus did claim to be Jehovah God. His affirmations of deity were neither vague nor ambiguous and by no means misunderstood. He was in fact, "God in the flesh."

—Eddie Dalcour
of John Jacobs' "Power Team"*

*For more information, write Eddie Dalcour, P. O. Box 2128, Winnetka, CA, 91396-2128.

Notes

Chapter 1

1. Edwin Louis Cole, *Manhood 101* (Tulsa, Okla.: Honor Books, 1995), 105.

2. William J. Bennett, copyright 1992, *The De-Valuing of America* (New York: Simon & Schuster, 1992), 10; reprinted with the publisher's permission.

3. *Wall Street Journal*, 6 March 1996.

4. Bennett, *The De-Valuing of America*, 5.

Chapter 2

1. William J. Federer, *America's God & Country, Encyclopedia of Quotations* (Coppell, Tex.: Fame Publishing, 1994), 43.

2. Dr. David Barrett, "Status of Global Mission, 1993, in Context of 20th and 21st Centuries" *International Bulletin of Missionary Research* (Richmond, Va.), January 1993. Other surveys place the number of Christians at far less. But the point remains that born-again believers are a distinct minority.

3. Cole, *Manhood 101*, 8.

4. Jack Canfield and Mark Hansen, *Chicken Soup for the Soul* (Boca Raton, Fla.: Health Communications, Inc., 1993), 214.

Chapter 4

1. James Hewett, ed., © 1988, *Illustrations Unlimited* (Wheaton, Ill.: Tyndale House Publishers, 1988), 452; used by permission; all rights reserved.

Chapter 5

1. Federer, *America's God & Country*, 473.

2. William J. Bennett, compiler, *The Moral Compass* (New York: Simon & Schuster, 1995), 594.

3. Van Crouch, *Staying Power* (Honor Books, 1996), 21.

Chapter 6

1. Matthew Henry and Thomas Scott, *Commentary on the Holy Bible* (Nashville, Tenn.: Thomas Nelson Publishers, 1979).

2. Federer, *America's God & Country*, 67.

3. Marshall Foster, *The American Covenant* (Thousand Oaks, Calif.: Mayflower Institute, 1993), 15.

4. *Voice* magazine (Costa Mesa, Calif.), March 1993, 8.

5. *The Rebirth of America* (Bala Cynwyd, Pa.: Arthur S. DeMoss Foundation,1986), 211.

6. Ibid., 35.

7. Federer, *America's God & Country*, 678.

8. Ibid., 181.

Chapter 7

1. Cole, *Manhood 101*, 101.

2. Van Crouch, *Winning 101* (Honor Books, 1995), 142.

3. Cole, *Manhood 101*, 9.

4. *New York Times* article which appeared in the *Orange County Register* (Orange, Calif.), 12 November 1995.

5. Hewett, *Illustrations Unlimited*, 195.

6. Dr. Larry Poland, *The Mediator* newsletter, vol. 9, no. 2 (Redlands, Calif.: Mastermedia International, 1-800-447-8711); reprinted by permission.

7. Cole, *Manhood 101*, 44–45.

8. Edwin Louis Cole, *Maximized Manhood* (Springdale, Pa.: Whitaker House, 1982), 77.

Chapter 8

1. Porter B. Williamson, *Patton's Principles* (Tucson, Ariz.: Management & Systems Consultants, 1979), 152.

2. Our close friend and noted author, Dennis Peacocke, first told me the story of being wary of rubbing a cat's fur in the wrong direction. You can contact Dennis at Strategic Christian Services, 1221 Farmers Lane, #B, Santa Rosa, CA 95405, 707-578-7700.

3. Crouch, *Staying Power*, 59.

Chapter 9

1. Crouch, *Staying Power*, 75.

2. *Motivational Quotes* (Lombard, Ill.: Great Quotations, Inc., 1984), 70.

3. D. James Kennedy's newsletter, published by Coral Ridge Ministries (Fort Lauderdale, Fla.), 22 December 1995.

4. "Not Just Politics as Usual," *George*, June/July 1996, 130.

5. *National & International Religion Report* (Roanoke, Va.) 19 February 1996, 1.

6. *Los Angeles Times*, 12 January 1996, C-1 and C-4.

7. Information from *New York Times* story that appeared in the *Orange County Register*, 12 January 1996, 3.

8. Ibid.

9. Cole, *Manhood 101*, 147.

10. Crouch, *Staying Power*, 11.

Chapter 10

1. Earl Creps, "Mr. Average," *Pentecostal Evangel* (Springfield, Mo.), 7 March 1993, 5–6.

2. Mike Barnicle, "Excuses, Excuses" *Boston Globe* story as published in the *Orange County Register*, 21 January 1996, 1–2.

3. Jim Rohn, *The Treasury of Quotes* (Irving, Texas: Jim Rohn International, 1994), 214.

Chapter 11

1. Bill McCartney, *From Ashes to Glory,* rev. ed. (Nashville, Tenn.: Thomas Nelson Publishers, 1995), 10–11.
2. Edwin Louis Cole, *Strong Men in Tough Times* (Lake Mary, Fla.: Creation House, 1993), 85–86.

Chapter 12

1. Gary Beasley, *The Conquering Church* (Lake Tahoe, Calif.: Christian Equippers International, 1989), 53–54. Story originally appeared in "The Life of Clebe McClary," published by The American Tract Society. Used with permission of Clebe McClary.
2. Henry Blackaby and Claude King, *Experiencing God* (Nashville, Tenn.: Broadman & Holman, 1994), 103.
3. Beasley, *The Conquering Church,* 53.
4. Federer, *America's God & Country,* 183–84.